1860 CENSUS

OF

FENTRESS COUNTY TENNESSEE

Transcribed by

Gerald R. Ramsey

Heritage Books
2026

HERITAGE BOOKS

AN IMPRINT OF HERITAGE BOOKS, INC.

Books, CDs, and more—Worldwide

For our listing of thousands of titles see our website
at
www.HeritageBooks.com

A Facsimile Reprint
Published 2026 by
HERITAGE BOOKS, INC.
Publishing Division
5810 Ruatan Street
Berwyn Heights, MD 20740

Transcribed from Microfilm
October 5, 1994
by Gerald R. Ramsey

Heritage Books by the author:
1860 Census of Fentress County, Tennessee
1920 Census of Fentress County, Tennessee

International Standard Book Number
Paperbound: 978-0-7884-8823-8

Index to Districts

1860 Fentress Co. TN Census

Name		Age Remarks	Sex	Race	Profession	Birth Place

Town of Jamestown
Recorded 23 June 1860

Name		Age	Sex	Race	Profession	Birth Place
Hildreth,	R. T.	32	M	W	Lawyer	IN
	Mary A.	26	F	W		TN
	Laura L.	5	F	W		TN, Jamestown
	Orian	3	M	W		TN, Jamestown
	Pearson	1	M	W		TN, Jamestown
Clark,	Levi	55	M	W	Hatter	NC
	Jane	47	F	W		NC
Rains,	Celia J.	9	F	W		TN
Paul,	Edley	36	M	W	Trader	VA
	Mary	32	F	W		TN
	Elizabeth	14	F	W		TN
	John M.	12	M	W		TN
	Mary B.	10	F	W		TN
	Charles T.	8	M	W		TN
	George H.	6	M	W		TN
	Joseph	5	M	W		TN
	Alice	2	F	W		TN
	Jane	2/12	F	W		TN
Simpson,	B. D.	29	M	W	Froder	TN
	Elizabeth	55	F	W	Domestic	MO
Lee,	B.	35	M	W		TN
	Catharine	22	F	W		TN
	Marvin B.	11	M	W		TN
	William	1	M	W		TN
Albertson,	John	23	M	W	Carpenter	TN
	Naoma	24	F	W		TN
Simpson,	J. G.	33	M	W	Jailer	TN
	Mary A.	28	F	W		TN
	Sarah J.	11	F	W		TN
	Mary M.	9	F	W		TN
	George W.	8	M	W		TN
	Unnamed	1	M	W		TN

1860 Fentress Co. TN Census

Name		Age Remarks	Sex	Race	Profession	Birth Place	

Town of Jamestown
Recorded 23 June 1860

Name		Age	Sex	Race	Profession	Birth Place	
Upchurch,	G. W.	29	M	W	Circuit Court Clerk		KY
	Sarah J.	23	F	W		TN	
	Samantha D.	5	F	W		TN	
	Victoria F.	2	F	W		TN	
Lee,	Matilda	60	F	W	Gardening	VA	
	Eliza J.	24	F	W		TN	
	Elizabeth H.	19	F			TN	
Livington,	John	25	M	W	Blacksmith	TN	
	Jane	20	F	W		TN	
	Flora A.	1/12	F	W		TN	
Crazin,	Ethellent	26	M	W	Merchant	TN	
Wright,	M.	30	M	W	Grocer	TN	
	Amanda	28	F	W		KY	
Wood,	Mary	50	F	W	Domestic	NC	
Simpson,	Roan	18	F	W	Domestic	TN	
	Hiram	22	M	W	Day Laborer	TN	
	Elizabeth	6	F	W		TN	
Kingston,	G. S.	52	M	W	County Register	TN	
	Melissa	35	F	W		TN	
	John H.	16	M	F		IL	
Morgan,	Julia A.	42	F	W	Tailoress	NC	
	William E.	13	M	W		TN	
	John	9	M	W		TN	
	Emeline	5	F	W		TN	
Bledsoe,	Sarah	36	F	W	Domestic	TN	
	John H.	14	M	W		TN	
	Mary E.	13	F	W		TN	
	Sarah J.	10	F	W		TN	
	Patience M.	9	F	W		TN	
	William B.	7	M	W		TN	
	W. A.	5	M	W		TN	
	Robert B.	3	M	W		TN	
	Julia A.	1	F	W		TN	

1860 Fentress Co. TN Census

Name		Age Remarks	Sex	Race	Profession	Birth Place

Town of Jamestown
Recorded 23 June 1860

Name		Age	Sex	Race	Profession	Birth Place
Stockton,	Isaac	57	M	W	Wool Corder	KY
	Mary A.	27	F	W		KY
	Richard	11	M	W		TN
	John R.	2	M	W		KY
	Martha C.	10/12	F	W		TN
Gray,	Felle	21	M	W		TN
Richardson,	Caroline	18	F	W		TN
Bledsoe,	B. F.	29	M	W	Lawyer	TN
	Margaret W.	25	F	W		TN
	C. T.	22	M	W	Constable	TN
	Rebeccah S.	20	F	W	Domestic	KY
Bledsoe,	R. H.	32	M	W	Lawyer	KY
	Icy	25	M	W		TN
	Josephine	8	F	W		TN
	Franklin	6	M	W		TN
	Mary	3	F	W		TN
	Viola	6/12	F	W		TN
Blakly,	Elizabeth	14	F	W	Domestic	TN
Gaudin,	J. W.	29	M	W	Merchant	Switzerland
	Adele	18	F	W		Switzerland
	Fanny	2	F	W		TN
	J. W.	1	M	W		TN
	Charles	13	M	W		Switzerland
Erwin,	W. H.	38	M	W	Merchant	TN
Conatser,	David	32	M	W	Tavern Keeper	TN
	Melissa	24	F	W		TN
	Milton	6	M	W		TN
	Amanda E.	4	F	W		TN
	Fletcher B.	3	M	W		TN
Wood,	Winnie	59	F	W	Domestic	TN
Sherrill,	Emma	20	F	W	Domestic	TN
	Jonathan S.	1	M	W		TN
Halt,	Lifus	24	M	W	Day Laborer	KY
	Jernsa	22	F	W		KY

1860 Fentress Co. TN Census

Name		Age Remarks	Sex	Race	Profession	Birth Place

Civil District No. 1
Recorded 6 June 1860

Name		Age	Sex	Race	Profession	Birth Place
Owen,	Joshua	61	M	W	Farmer	SC
	Mary	56	F	W		KY
	John F.	34	M	W	Farmer	TN
Cobb,	Jessie Jr.	26	M	W	Farmer	TN
	Phebe	22	F	W		TN
	Cavena	4	F	W		TN
	Scott	3/12	M	W		TN
Franklin,	Handley?	22	M	W	Laborer	TN
Beaty,	Thomas	59	M	W	Farmer	TN
	Jane	55	F	W		KY
	Thomas J.	22	M	W	Farmer	TN
	William N.	13	M	W	Farmer	TN
	Matilda	11	F	W		TN
	Hirma C.	9	M	W		TN
Smith,	George	50	M	W	Farmer	TN
	Bethena	43	F	W		TN
	John C.	18	M	W	Farmer	TN
	Elizabeth	17	F	W		TN
	George W.	14	M	W		TN
Hill,	Robert C.	49	M	W	Farmer	TN
	Anna A.	43	F	W		TN
	Matilda J.	23	F	W		TN
	Mary W.	21	F	W		TN
	Melissa E.	19	F	W		TN
Benton,	John	16	M	W	Farmer	TN
	Sida E.	14	F	W		TN
	Laura E.	11	F	W		TN
	Adela A.	9	F	W		TN
	Susan Celle	7	F	W		TN
	Martha E.	4	F	W		TN
	Lucinda A.	1	F	W		TN
	Margaret S.	5	F	W		TN

1860 Fentress Co. TN Census

Name		Age Remarks	Sex	Race	Profession	Birth Place

Civil District No. 1
Recorded 7 June 1860

Name		Age Remarks	Sex	Race	Profession	Birth Place
Wood,	William W.	30	M	W	Farmer	TN
	Elizabeth J.	25	F	W		TN
	Cinthia C.	12	F	W		TN
	Mary J.	10	F	W		TN
	Elizabeth	8	F	W		TN
	Abigail	7	F	W		TN
	A. M.	5	F	W		TN
	John B.	4	M	W		TN
	Douglas	7/12	M	W		TN
Beaty,	Jeremiah	40	M	W	Farmer	TN
	Sarah	27	F	W		TN
	Henry T.	8	M	W		TN
	Jacob	7	M	W		TN
	Vienna	?	F	W		TN
	Nancy A.	9/12	F	W		TN
Beaty,	Sarah	65	F	W	Farmer	VA
	Nancy	27	F	W		TN
	Artemia	26	F	W		TN
Reagan,	Elizabeth	23	F	W	Domestic	TN
Conatser,	John	24	M	W	Farmer	TN
Beaty,	David	45	M	W	Farmer	TN
	Jane	30	F	W		TN
	Catherine	15	F	W		TN
	Lodicia	13	F	W		TN
	Richard	11	M	W		TN
	Martin	9	M	W		TN
	Andrew C.	6	M	W		TN
	Julia Ann	4	F	W		TN
	John	2	M	W		TN

1860 Fentress Co. TN Census

Name		Age Remarks	Sex	Race	Profession	Birth Place

Civil District No. 1
Recorded 7 June 1860

Name		Age	Sex	Race	Profession	Birth Place
Beaty,	David Sr.	43	M	W	Farmer	TN
	Ava	39	F	W		TN
	James M.	17	M	W	Farmer	TN
	Claiborne	15	M	W	Farmer	TN
	Hevaey	12	M	W		TN
	John C.	9	M	W		TN
	William J.	4	M	W		TN
Stephens,	Rae	20	M	W	Day Laborer	TN
Choate,	Austin	65	M	W	Farmer	NC
	Elizabeth	55	F	W		TN
	John	19	M	W	Farmer	TN
	Christopher	18	M	W	Farmer	TN
	Lademia	16	F	W		TN
	Christopher	85	M	W	Farming	VA
Choate,	Jacob	30	M	W	Farming	TN
	Margaret	30	F	W		KY
	Saberm	10	M	W		TN
	Sarah	7	F	W		TN
	George	5	M	W		TN
	Sarah	35	F	W	Domestic	KY
Beaty,	Mary	50	F	W	Domestic	TN
Linder,	Thomas	39	M	W	Farmer	TN
	Anna	37	F	W		TN
	John	14	M	W		TN
	Catherine	12	F	W		TN
	Dawson	10	M	W		TN
	Edley	8	M	W		TN
	Matilda	6	F	W		TN
	Mary A.	1	F	W		TN
Linder,	George	19	M	W	Farmer	TN
	Fanny	25	F	W		TN

<u>1860 Fentress Co. TN Census</u>

Name		Age Remarks	Sex	Race	Profession	Birth Place

Civil District No. 1
Recorded 7 June 1860

Name		Age Remarks	Sex	Race	Profession	Birth Place
Beaty,	James	23	M	W	Farmer	TN
	Amilda	20	F	W		TN
	Cinthia	1	F	W		TN
	Unnamed	1/12	F	W		TN
Mullinix,	Eli	45	M	W	Farmer	TN
	Inglingtine	37	F	W		TN
	Benton	17	M	W	Farmer	TN
	Elizabeth	14	F	W		TN
York,	Thomas	57	M	W	Farmer	TN
	Margaret	24	F	W		TN
	Milly	14	F	W		TN
	Caleb	12	M	W		TN
	Jackson	11	M	W		TN
	Mary E.	8	F	W		TN
	Visa A.	6	F	W		TN
	James T.	2	M	W		TN
York,	Mitchel	19	M	W	Day Laborer	TN
	Sarah A.	19	F	W		KY
Baily,	Champ	45	M	W	Laborer	VA
	Christina	47	F	W		KY
	Elizabeth	18	F	W		KY
	Eliza J.	15	F	W		KY
	William G.	12	M	W		KY
	Nancy C.	6	F	W		KY
	Samuel J.	2	M	W		KY
York,	Jefferson	22	M	W	Day Laborer	TN
	Married within					
	Lucinda	18	F	W		TN the
year						
Owens,	Jeremiah	37	M	W	Farmer	TN
	Minerva	34	F	W		TN
	George W.	17	M	W		TN
	Nancy J.	14	F	W		TN
	Sarah E.	14	F	W		TN
	Margaret	11	F	W		TN
	Canzada	5/12	F	W		TN

1860 Fentress Co. TN Census

Name		Age Remarks	Sex	Race	Profession	Birth Place

Civil District No. 1
Recorded 7 June 1860

Name		Age	Sex	Race	Profession	Birth Place
Turner,	McKayer	38	M	W	Tenant	TN
	Mary	38	F	W		TN
	James	18	M	W	Tenant	TN
	John	16	M	W	Tenant	TN
	Francis	14	M	W		TN
	Thomas G.	13	M	W		TN
	Eliza A.	11	F	W		TN
	Charles P.	7	M	W		TN
	Melissa M.	5	F	W		TN
	William	3	M	W		TN
	Artemia	1/12	F	W		TN
York,	Mary E.	5	F	W		TN
Soloman,	Sanford J.	47	M	W	Miller	NC
	Anna	36	F	W		TN
	Artemia C.	9	F	W		TN
	Ethelert C.	7	M	W		TN
	Thomas F.	5	M	W		TN
	David C.	4	M	W		TN
	Nancy E.	3	F	W		TN
	Sarah R.	1	F	W		TN
Hampton,	Zachariah	41	M	W	Mechanic	KY
	Sarah M.	32	F	W		VA
	John H.	11	M	W		KY
	William	8	M	W		TN
	James D.	6	M	W		KY
	Thomas	3	M	W		KY
	Bailey	3/12	M	W		TN
Whited,	Robert	59	M	W	Farmer	KY
	Jane	60	F	W		VA
	Matilda	19	F	W		VA
	Sarah	16	F	W		VA

1860 Fentress Co. TN Census

Name		Age Remarks	Sex	Race	Profession	Birth Place

Civil District No. 1
Recorded 7 June 1860

Name		Age	Sex	Race	Profession	Birth Place
Owen,	Elias	27	M	W	Farmer	TN
	Ferila	25	F	W		TN
	John B.	3	M	W		TN
	James	2	M	W		TN
Conatser,	Philip	26	M	W	Tenant	TN
	Abigail B.	28	F	W		TN
	William A.	3	M	W		TN
	John L.	9/12	M	W		TN
Linder,	John	60	M	W	Merchant	TN
	Mary	59	F	W		SC
	John J.	20	M	W	Merchant	TN
	Sarah A.	24	F	W		TN
	George W.	16	M	W	Merchant	TN
Owen,	William P.	33	M	W	Farmer	TN
	Melissa	18	F	W		TN
	Abigail	11/12	F	W		TN
	James	26	M	W	Day Laborer	TN
Wood,	Isaac	26	M	W	Farmer	TN
	Sarah A.	24	F	W		TN
	Ardelia	4	F	W		TN
	Nancy J.	2	F	W		TN
	Florence F.	9/12	F	W		TN
Beaty,	Jeremiah	21	M	W	Tenant	TN
	Nancy	20	F	W		TN
Bowden,	Elias	67	M	W	Farmer	TN
	Mary	56	F	W		TN
	Elias W.	30	M	W	Farmer	TN
	Emma	22	F	W		TN
	Lylian B.	11/12	F	W		TN
	John W.	17	M	W	Farmer	TN

1860 Fentress Co. TN Census

Name		Age Remarks	Sex	Race	Profession	Birth Place

Civil District No. 1
Recorded 7 June 1860

Name		Age Remarks	Sex	Race	Profession	Birth Place
Owen,	James B.	35	M	W	Day Laborer	TN
	Rodecka A.	32	F	W		TN
	Mathew	9	M	W		TN
	Margaret	6	F	W		TN
	Sarah K.	1	F	W		TN
Beaty,	Fleming	48	M	W	Farmer	TN
	Sarah	44	F	W		TN
	Lydia	19	F	W		TN
	Balaam	13	M	W		TN
	Jesse	11	M	W		TN
	Fanny	8	F	W		TN
	James	6	M	W		TN
	Mary	4	F	W		TN
	David	1	M	W		TN
Beaty,	John	21	M	W	Tenant	TN
	Vilena	21	F	W		TN
	Vernetta	2	F	W		TN
	A.	11/12	M	W		TN
Stephens,	William	18	M	W	Day Laborer	TN
Wright,	Jacob	37	M	W	Farmer	TN
	America	30	F	W		TN
	James	11	M	W		TN
	Nina J.	10	F	W		TN
	William	8	M	W		TN
	Simon	7	M	W		TN
	Joseph	5	M	W		TN
	Margaret	3	F	W		TN
	Emma	1	F	W		TN
Ferrell,	David	37	M	W	Tenant	TN
	Nancy	37	F	W		TN
	James	13	M	W		TN
	William H.	11	M	W		TN
	Jane	5	F	W		TN
	George	4	M	W		TN
	Samuel	3	M	W		TN
	John	5 days	M	W		TN

1860 Fentress Co. TN Census

Name		Age Remarks	Sex	Race	Profession	Birth Place

Civil District No. 1
Recorded 7 June 1860

Name		Age	Sex	Race	Profession	Birth Place
Wright,	William	30	M	W		TN
	Matilda	22	F	W		TN
	Fanny	1	F	W		TN
--?--,	Elizabeth	12	F	W	Domestic	TN
Block,	George D.	26	M	W	Farmer	TN
	Margaret	36	F	W		TN
Wright,	Samuel	50	M	W	Farmer	VA
	Celia	40	F	W		TN
	Silas	16	M	W	Farmer	TN
	Mahala	13	F	W		TN
	Sarah	12	F	W		TN
	Margaret	9	F	W		TN
	Samuel	4	M	W		TN
Smith,	David	42	M	W	Farmer	TN
	Fanny	38	F	W		TN
	Ahijah	17	M	W	Farmer	TN
	Asa	16	M	W	Farmer	TN
	Elander J.	14	F	W		TN
	Deborah	11	F	W		TN
	Sarah E.	6	F	W		TN
	Genetta C.	5	F	W		TN
King,	Jeremiah	19	M	W	Tenant	TN
	Ruth	26	F	W		TN
	Ada	4	F	W		TN
Albertson,	Rachel	50	F	W		TN
Block,	Elizabeth	47	F	W	Gardening	KY
Walker,	Evander	28	M	W	Farmer	TN
	Mary	29	F	W		TN
	Nancy A.	7	F	W		TN
	John	5	M	W		TN
	William	4	M	W		TN
	George	1	M	W		TN
Price,	Sarah	48	F	W	Farming	TN
	James	19	M	W	Farming	TN
	George	9	M	W		TN

1860 Fentress Co. TN Census

Name		Age Remarks	Sex	Race	Profession	Birth Place	

Civil District No. 1
Recorded 9 June 1860

Name		Age	Sex	Race	Profession	Birth Place	
Albertson,	Isaac	30	M	W	Day Laborer	TN	
	Martha J.	23	F	W		TN	
	Sarah A.	3	F	W		TN	
	Soloman	9/12	M	W		TN	
Cooper,	Conncal	26	M	W	Blacksmith	TN	
	Nancy	24	F	W		TN	
	James	2	M	W		FN	
	Henry L.	1	M	W		TN	
Bruce,	John T.	40	M	W	Tenant	TN	
	Mary	36	F	W		TN	
	Nancy	14	F	W		TN	
	James	4	M	W		TN	
King,	John	64	M	W	Farmer	TN	
	Anna	54	F	W		TN	
	Henry	16	M	W	Farmer	TN	
	Lucinda	24	F	W	Farmer	TN	
	Louisa	30	F	W	Domestic	TN	
	Thomas	16	M	W	Farming	TN	
	Mary	15	F	W		TN	
	Jane	12	F	W		TN	
	Joel	22	M	W		TN	
King,	Thomas	22	M	W	Tenant	TN	
	Ellen	20	F	W		TN	
	Henry	2	M	W		TN	
King,	Jackson	21	M	W	Tenant	TN	
	Married within						
	Mary	22	F	W		TN	the
year							
	John	1	M	W		TN	
King,	John Jr.	34	M	W	Tenant	TN	
	Louisa	30	F	W		TN	
	June	14	F	W		TN	
	John	13	M	W		TN	
	Nancy A.	8/12	F	W		TN	

1860 Fentress Co. TN Census

Name		Age Remarks	Sex	Race	Profession	Birth Place

Civil District No. 1
Recorded 9 June 1860

Name		Age	Sex	Race	Profession	Birth Place
King,	Jeremiah B.	20	M	W	Tenant	TN
	Ruth	30	F	W		TN
	Albert C.	2	M	W		TN
Albertson,	Rachel	65	F	W	Obstetrician	TN
King,	William	26	M	W	Farmer	TN
	Mary	29	F	W		TN
	Catharine	1	F	W		TN
Wright,	John	42	M	W	Farmer	TN
	Mary	35	F	W		TN
	William J.	17	M	W	Farmer	TN
	Jesse L.	15	M	W	Farmer	TN
	Arissa J.	14	F	W		TN
	Noah	12	M	W		TN
	Martha A.	10	F	W		TN
Owen,	William	54	M	W	Master Mason	NC
	Mary J.	23	F	W		TN
	James W.	21	M	W	Day Laborer	TN
	John R.	17	M	W	Day Laborer	TN
	Susanah M.	15	F	W		TN
	George B.	14	M	W		TN
	Feriba	11	F	W		TN
	Margaret	9	F	W		TN
Price,	Nancy	58	F	W	Tenant	TN
	Elizabeth	29	F	W		TN
	John	27	M	W	Shoe Maker	TN
	Zileba	21	F	W		TN
	Thomas	18	M	W	Tenant	TN
	Nathaniel P.	15	M	W	Tenant	TN
Cooper,	Jacob	29	M	W	Tenant	TN
	James	1	M	W		TN

1860 Fentress Co. TN Census

Name		Age Remarks	Sex	Race	Profession	Birth Place

Civil District No. 1
Recorded 9 June 1860

Name		Age	Sex	Race	Profession	Birth Place
Cooper,	Henry	45	M	W	Farming	TN
	Amanda	50	F	W		TN
	Elizabeth	22	F	W		TN
	Julia	20	F	W		TN
	Martha	18	F	W		TN
	Marie L.	16	F	W		TN
	Jane	14	F	W		TN
	Alexander	12	M	W		TN
	Simon P.	9	M	W		TN
	Henry	8	M	W		TN
Franklin,	George W.	29	M	W	Farmer	TN
	Dice	24	F	W		TN
	Jesse	4	M	W		TN
	John	3	M	W		TN
	James	4/12	M	W		TN
Franklin,	Edward	53	M	W	Farmer	TN
	Sarah	49	F	W		TN
	Alsa	32	F	W		TN
	Thomas S.	21	M	W	Farmer	TN
	Edward	16	M	W	Farmer	TN
	William	13	M	W		TN
	Jane	11	F	W		TN
Cooper,	John	60	M	W	Tenant	TN
	Louisa	36	F	W		TN
	James O.	10	M	W		TN
	Alsa A.	7	F	W		TN
	Nancy M.	4	F	W		TN
Cooper,	Jacob	49	M	W	Farmer	KY
	Catharine	40	F	W		TN
	Jeremiah	17	M	W	Farmer	TN
	Thomas	15	M	W	Farmer	TN
	Sarah	13	F	W		TN
	Cuzza	11	F	W		TN
	David	9	M	W		TN
	William	7	M	W		TN
	George	4	M	W		TN
	Artemia	2	F	W		TN
	Julia E.	5/12	F	W		TN
	Canncil	65	M	W	Day Laborer	TN

1860 Fentress Co. TN Census

Name		Age Remarks	Sex	Race	Profession	Birth Place

Civil District No. 1
Recorded 11 June 1860

Name		Age Remarks	Sex	Race	Profession	Birth Place
Robbins,	Mary	42	F	W	Farming	TN
	John	19	M	W	Farming	TN
	George	16	M	W	Farming	TN
	Nancy	15	F	W		TN
	Alfred	11	M	W		TN
	Fanny E.	7	F	W		TN
	James	5	M	W		TN
	Emma	3	F	W		TN
	Rachel	21	F	W	Domestic	TN
Robbins,	Isaac J.	21	M	W	Tenant	TN
	Mary	17	F	W		TN
	Susanah E.	3/12	F	W		TN
Winningham, Jane		44	F	W	Tenant	TN
	Margaret	18	F	W		TN
	Soloman	17	M	W	Day Laborer	TN
	Maria	12	F	W		TN
	Richard A.	10	M	W		TN
	Susa E.	3	F	W		TN
Conatser,	John E.	21	M	W	Tenant	TN
	Winnie	18	F	W		TN
Ledbetter,	Brasley	58	M	W	Farmer	GA
	Susanah	52	F	W		TN
	Ewing Mc	13	M	W		TN
	Barther	10	F	W		TN
	Artilla	7	F	W		TN
Robbins,	Marshall L.	22	M	W	Tenant	TN
	Louisa	24	F	W		TN
	Malvina	5	F	W		TN
Franklin,	Clark	22	M	W	Tenant	TN
	Martha	22	F	W		TN
	James C.	3	M	W		TN
	Julia L.	1	F	W		TN

1860 Fentress Co. TN Census

Name		Age Remarks	Sex	Race	Profession	Birth Place

Name		Age	Sex	Race	Profession	Birth Place
Ledbetter,	James W.	25	M	W	Farmer	TN
	Elizabeth	24	F	W		TN
	Buckner H.	6	M	W		TN
	Nancy J.	4	F	W		TN
	George	3	M	W		TN
	James W.	1	M	W		TN
	Arthur A.	7/12	M	W		TN
	Nancy	18	F	W	Domestic	TN
Smith,	Henry	42	M	W	Farmer	TN
Sells,	Thomas	21	M	W		TN
	Lena	23	F	W		TN
	Sarah	10/12	F	W		TN
Cravens,	Margaret	55	F	W	Tenant	TN
	Elliot	26	M	W	Tenant	TN
	Rhoda A.	21	F	W		TN
	Lena	18	F	W		TN
	Lean E. J.	16	F	W		TN
	William J.	14	M	W		TN
	Sarah C.	12	F	W		TN
Sells,	William	31	M	W	Farmer	VA
	Matilda J.	24	F	W		TN
	Lafayette	4	M	W		TN
	George	2	M	W		TN
Hollent,	Nathaniel	20	M	W	Day Laborer	TN

1860 Fentress Co. TN Census

Name		Age Remarks	Sex	Race	Profession	Birth Place

Civil District No. 1
Recorded 11 June 1860

Name		Age	Sex	Race	Profession	Birth Place
Gunter,	William	50	M	W	Farmer	TN
	Cinthia S.	50	F	W		TN
	George W.	20	M	W	Farmer	TN
	Lucinda	17	F	W		TN
	John	16	M	W	Farmer	TN
	William	14	M	W		TN
	James	12	M	W		TN
	Mary	8	F	W		TN
Price,	Eliza	28	F	W	Domestic	KY
	Samantha E.	5	F	W		TN
	Melissa E.	4	F	W		TN
Huddleston,	Thomas	49	M	W	Tenant	TN
	Matilda	50	F	W		TN
	Joel G.	14	M	W		TN
	William E.	9	M	W		TN
Huddleston,	John	77	M	W	Farmer	VA
	Joel G.	42	M	W	Farmer	TN
	Tennessee	41	F	W		TN
	James	8	M	W		TN
	William	5	M	W		TN
	Bonnapart	3	M	W		TN
	Demetrious	9/12	M	W		TN
Beaty,	George	45	M	W	Farmer	TN
	Annes	50	F	W		TN
	Margaret	55	F	W	Domestic	TN

Recorded 12 June 1860

Name		Age	Sex	Race	Profession	Birth Place
Conatser,	Philip	45	M	W	Farmer	TN
	Mary	28	F	W		TN
	William	8	M	W		TN
	June	6	F	W		TN
	Sarah	4	F	W		TN
	John	1	M	W		TN
Wood,	Lulu	26	F	W	Domestic	TN

1860 Fentress Co. TN Census

Name		Age Remarks	Sex	Race	Profession	Birth Place

Civil District No. 1
Recorded 12 June 1860

Name		Age	Sex	Race	Profession	Birth Place
Beaty,	N. P.	25	M	W	Tenant	TN
	Ellen	21	F	W		TN
Beaty,	Andrew	57	M	W	Farmer	KY
	Mary A. L.	44	F	W		TN
	Elizabeth	19	F	W		TN
	Zilpha J.	17	F	W		TN
	William E.	15	M	W		TN
	Abram	10	M	W		TN
	Nancy A. L.	8	F	W		TN
King,	James	45	M	W	Farmer	TN
	Elizabeth	38	F	W		KY
	William G.	16	M	W	Farmer	TN
	Martha J.	15	F	W		TN
	Nancy E.	13	F	W		TN
	Mahala	11	F	W		TN
	Thomas J.	10	M	W		TN
	Andrew J.	2	M	W		TN
	Tennessee	4/12	M	W		TN
Cooper,	Caraway	35	M	W	Tenant	TN
	Manirva	32	F	W		TN
	David	12	M	W		TN
	Thomas	9	M	W		TN
	William	7	M	W		TN
	Elizabeth	4	F	W		TN
	Mahala	2	F	W		TN
Hinds,	Nina	57	F	W	Tenant	TN
	Simon	26	M	W	Tenant	TN
	Isham	22	M	W	Day Laborer	TN
	Joel	20	M	W	Day Laborer	TN
	Penny	18	M	W	Day Laborer	TN
	Nina J.	15	F	W		TN

1860 Fentress Co. TN Census

Name		Age Remarks	Sex	Race	Profession	Birth Place	

Civil District No. 1
Recorded 12 June 1860

Name		Age	Sex	Race	Profession	Birth Place	
Hill,	Andrew B.	30	M	W	Farmer	KY	
	Caroline	24	F	W		TN	
	Nathan J.	1	M	W		TN	
Smith,	Allen A.	23	M	W	Tenant	TN	
	Sarah	23	F	W		TN	
	Marvin	6/12	M	W		TN	
Hoover,	Henry	26	M	W	Tenant	TN	
	Mary A.	26	F	W		TN	
	Sarah	4	F	W		TN	
	Rice	10/12	M	W		TN	
Hoover,	Catharine	55	F	W	Tenant	TN	
	Jane	12	F	W		TN	
Gooding,	Nicholas	53	M	W	Tenant	TN	
	Margaret	55	F	W		TN	
	Andrew A.	27	M	W	Day Laborer	TN	
	James H.	26	M	W	Day Laborer	TN	
	Martha J.	22	F	W		TN	
	Mary A.	19	F	W		TN	
Stephens,	Phebe	47	F	W	Tenant	TN	
	Squire	14	M	W		TN	
	Jeremiah	13	M	W		TN	
	Celia	11	F	W		TN	
	David	6	M	W		TN	
	Nancy	4	F	W		TN	
Smith,	Silas	34	M	W	Farmer	TN	
	Margaret	33	F	W		TN	
	William	13	M	W		TN	
	Celia J.	12	F	W		TN	Deaf &
Dumb							
	John	10	M	W		TN	
	Soloman	8	M	W		TN	
	Sarah E.	1	F	W		TN	

1860 Fentress Co. TN Census

Name		Age Remarks	Sex	Race	Profession	Birth Place
		Civil District No. 1				
		Recorded 12 June 1860				
Smith,	Richard M.	25	M	W	Tenant	TN
	Nancy	18	F	W		TN
Stephens,	John	28	M	W	Farmer	TN
	Matilda	30	F	W		TN
	Hatty J.	9	F	W		TN
	William	5	M	W		TN
	Celia	2	F	W		TN
Whited,	James	37	M	W	Farmer	TN
	Larassa	39	F	W		TN
	Lydia	16	F	W		TN
	John R.	13	M	W		TN
	Elender J.	12	F	W		TN
	Mary A. T.	9	F	W		TN
	William W.	9/12	M	W		TN
Franklin,	James	35	M	W	Tenant	TN
	Mahala	31	F	W		TN
	Thomas	12	M	W		TN
	Margaret J.	10	F	W		TN
	Nancy E.	8	F	W		TN
	David	5	M	W		TN
	James B.	4	M	W		TN
	John	9/12	M	W		TN
Franklin,	Nathan	38	M	W	Farmer	TN
	Kiziah	49	F	W		TN
	John	10	M	W		TN
Franklin,	Isaac	72	M	W	Tenant	NC
	Nancy	59	F	W		SC
Whited,	Francis	39	M	W	Farmer	TN
	Elizabeth	29	F	W		VA
	Jane	13	F	W		TN
	Armilda	12	F	W		TN
	Ellen	10	F	W		TN
	Robert	8	M	W		TN
	Rachel	5	F	W		TN
	Nancy	3	F	W		TN

1860 Fentress Co. TN Census

Name		Age Remarks	Sex	Race	Profession	Birth Place

Civil District No. 1
Recorded 13 June 1860

Name		Age	Sex	Race	Profession	Birth Place
Smith,	John	30	M	W	Farmer	TN
	Mary	30	F	W		TN
	William	10	M	W		TN
	Susanah	8	F	W		TN
	Isaac	6	M	W		TN
	Sarah	4	F	W		TN
	James	6/12	M	W		TN
	Lydia	70	F	W	Domestic	TN
Turner,	Thomas R.	30	M	W	Farmer	TN
	Eliza A.	29	F	W		IL
	John R.	10	M	W		TN
	Lean J.	8	F	W		TN
	Andrew J.	5	M	W		TN
	Matilda C.	1	F	W		TN
King,	Robert	40	M	W	Farmer	TN
	Nancy	35	F	W		TN
	Thomas G.	16	M	W	Farmer	TN
	James F.	15	M	W	Farmer	TN
	Peter P.	10	M	W	Farmer	TN
	Sarah J.	8	F	W		TN
	Elizabeth A.	6	F	W		TN
	Martha E.	3	F	W		TN
Reeder,	Joseph	37	M	W	Farmer	TN
	Sarah	39	F	W		VA
	Elizabeth	16	F	W		TN
	Mary	13	F	W		TN
	George	11	M	W		TN
	John	9	M	W		TN
	Heza Bioh?	7	M	W		TN
	John	5	M	W		TN
	Lean	2	F	W		TN

1860 Fentress Co. TN Census

Name		Age Remarks	Sex	Race	Profession	Birth Place

Civil District No. 2
Recorded 13 June 1860

Name		Age	Sex	Race	Profession	Birth Place	Remarks
Choate,	George	39	M	W	Tenant	AL	
	Milinda	38	F	W		TN	
	Lucy	12	F	W		TN	
	James W.	10	M	W		TN	
	Jacob	9	M	W		TN	
	John	8	M	W		TN	
	Elizabeth	7	F	W		TN	
	Mary A.	2	F	W		TN	
Albertson,	John	68	M	W	Farmer	NC	
	Martha	39	F	W		TN	
	Sarah	38	F	W		TN	
	Elizabeth	29	F	W		TN	
	Benj. H.	27	M	W		TN	
	Isaac D.	25	M	W		TN	
	Hannah	23	F	W		TN	
Albertson,	Elizabeth	66	F	W	Gardening	NC	
	Hannah	61	F	W		NC	Idiotic
Albertson,	E. W.	37	M	W		TN	
	Levina	32	F	W		TN	
Findley,	Benjamin	36	M	W	Farmer	TN	
	Susanah	38	F	W	Domestic	TN	
	Hiram	14	M	W	Farmer	TN	
Bronniss,	Mary	33	F	W	Tenant	TN	
	Bailor	10	M	W		TN	
	Elizabeth	8	F	W		TN	
Conatser,	G. W.	19	M	W	Farmer	TN	
	Elizabeth	24	F	W	Domestic	TN	
	Sarah	21	F	W		TN	
	Catharine	17	F	W		TN	

1860 Fentress Co. TN Census

Name		Age Remarks	Sex	Race	Profession	Birth Place

Civil District No. 2
Recorded 13 June 1860

Name		Age	Sex	Race	Profession	Birth Place
Conatser,	James J.	64	M	W	Wheel Wright	NC
	Agnes	65	F	W		NC
	Mary	29	F	W	Domestic	TN
	Emeline	24	F	W		TN
	Matilda J.	4	F	W		TN
	George F.	3	M	W		TN
	John E.	2	M	W		TN
						.
Bronniss,	Benjamin	56	M	W	Farmer	TN
	Mary	45	F	W		TN
	James	23	M	W		TN
	Benjamin	17	M	W		TN
	Joseph	17	M	W	Farmer	TN
	Margaret P.	19	F	W		TN
	Mary	14	F	W		TN
	Martha	12	F	W		TN
	John	6	M	W		TN
Crockett,	John	16	M	W	Day Laborer	TN
Crockett,	James B.	42	M	W		TN
	Catharine	39	F	W		TN
	Frances M.	16	M	W		TN
	Robert	9	M	W		TN
Doss,	Job	24	M	W	Farming	TN
Wright,	Wilson L.	50	M	W		NC
	Hannah	45	F	W		TN
	Joshua F.	21	M	W	Farming	TN
	Boswell F.	17	M	W		TN
	Lewis W.	14	M	W		TN
	Margaret E. C.	12	F	W		TN
	Pamela A. C.	10	F	W		TN
	Unnamed	9/12	F	W		TN
Wright,	John C.	27	M	W	Farmer	TN
Albertson,	Jane	24	F	W	Domestic	TN
	Calvin M.	7	M	W		TN
	William H.	6	M	W		TN
	Patrick H.	5	M	W		TN
	Hannah E.	4	F	W		TN
Paul,	Margaret	18	F	W	Domestic	TN

1860 Fentress Co. TN Census

Name		Age Remarks	Sex	Race	Profession	Birth Place	

Civil District No. 2
Recorded 13 June 1860

Name		Age	Sex	Race	Profession	Birth Place	
Paul,	W. B.	27	M	W	Tenant	TN	
	Married within						
	Sarah A. C.	21	F	W		TN	the
year							
	Catharine	23	F	W	Domestic	TN	
Wright,	Alexander	40	M	W	Farmer	TN	
	Rachel	16	F	W		TN	
	Mary	14	F	W		TN	
	Joshua	12	M	W		TN	
	James	10	M	W		TN	
	Elizabeth	7	F	W		TN	
Hays,	Jonathan	39	M	W	Farmer	TN	
	Jane	33	F	W		TN	
	W. A.	11	M	W		TN	
	Susanah C.	9	F	W		TN	
	Isaac L.	5	M	W		TN	
	Sarah E.	1	F	W		TN	

Recorded 14 June 1860

Name		Age	Sex	Race	Profession	Birth Place
Campbell,	Rhoda M.	57	F	W	Farming	KY
	J. J.	25	M	W		TN
	Elizabeth J.	22	F	W		TN
	Nancy S.	20	F	W		TN
	Joseph F.	15	M	W		TN
	Henderson M.	12	M	W		TN
	William	10	M	W		TN
	Rebeccah M.	8	F	W		TN
	Thomas M.	6	M	W		TN
	Milton V.	19	M	W	Day Laborer	TN
Robinson,	William B.	28	M	W	Tenant	TN
	Eliza J.	25	F	W		TN
	James G.	2	M	W		TN
	Mary E.	6/12	F	W		TN
Walker,	James P.	27	M	W	Tenant	TN
	Susanah	19	F	W		TN
	Margaret J.	3	F	W		TN
	Sarah E.	2/12	F	W		TN
	Margaret	60	F	W	Domestic	VA

1860 Fentress Co. TN Census

Name		Age Remarks	Sex	Race	Profession	Birth Place

Civil District No. 2
Recorded 14 June 1860

Name		Age	Sex	Race	Profession	Birth Place
McCollumn,	Isaac	65	M	W	Tenant	VA
	Nancy	50	F	W		TN
Cobb,	John	39	M	W	Farmer	TN
	Frances	40	F	W		TN
	Malvina	10	F	W		TN
	Mary A.	7	F	W		TN
	John A.	2	M	W		TN
Crabtree,	James	7	M	W		TN
Bronniss,	William	28	M	W	Tenant	TN
	Elizabeth	22	F	W		TN
	Edward	2	M	W		TN
Crockett,	Kenny	20	M	W	Day Laborer	TN
Lewallin,	Herrod	39	M	W	Tenant	TN
	Phebe	41	F	W		TN
	Andrew	20	M	W	Day Laborer	TN
	Miva A.	18	F	W		TN
	William	16	M	W		TN
	Amanda	13	F	W		TN
	Rufus	6	M	W		TN
	Vilma	3	F	W		TN
	Farzina	4/12	F	W		TN
Richardson,	H. H.	34	M	W	Farmer	TN
	Mary	28	F	W		TN
	Thursa E.	11	F	W		TN
	James M.	9	M	W		TN
	Nancy F.	7	F	W		TN
	Abigail T.	3	F	W		TN
Gray,	Nancy	63	F	W	Tenant	TN
	Nealy	10	F	W		TN

1860 Fentress Co. TN Census

Name		Age Remarks	Sex	Race	Profession	Birth Place

Civil District No. 2
Recorded 14 June 1860

Name		Age	Sex	Race	Profession	Birth Place
Paul,	William W.	37	M	W	Tenant	VA
	Margaret A.	32	F	W		TN
	Edley	12	M	W		TN
	John	10	M	W		TN
	Tabitha	9	F	W		TN
	Charles	7	M	W		TN
	Sarah J.	4	F	W		TN
	James	9/12	M	W		FN
Carpenter,	Consides	62	M	W	Farmer	MA
	Susanah	59	F	W		TN
	Lucinda J.	27	F	W		TN
	John R.	20	M	W		TN
Tipton,	William	29	M	W	Tenant	TN
	Susanah	29	F	W		TN
	Margaret	11	F	W		TN
	Eliza	9	F	W		TN
	Nancy	8	F	W		TN
	Littleton	6	M	W		TN
	William	4	M	W		TN
	Daniel	1	M	W		TN
Smith,	Tennessee	15	F	W	Domestic	TN
Mullinix,	Nathaniel	60	M	W	Farmer	TN
	Elizabeth	58	F	W		TN
	A. J.	21	M	W		TN
	Elizabeth	18	F	W		TN
	Isaac	15	M	W		TN
	Nancy	14	F	W		TN
	Nathaniel	12	M	W		TN
	Sarah	77	F	W	Domestic	TN
Carpenter,	George	21	M	W	Tenant	TN
	Eliza E.	21	F	W		TN
	Sarah J.	1	F	W		TN
York,	Amos	25	M	W	Tenant	TN
	Rhoda	24	F	W		TN
	Mary	4/12	F	W		TN

1860 Fentress Co. TN Census

Name		Age Remarks	Sex	Race	Profession	Birth Place

Civil District No. 2
Recorded 14 June 1860

Name		Age	Sex	Race	Profession	Birth Place
Choate,	Christopher	24	M	W	Tenant	TN
	Catharine	22	F	W		TN
	Celia A. C.	3	F	W		TN
	Edward J.	2	M	W		TN
	Nancy J.	3/12	F	W		TN
Millsap,	Marsha S.	55	F	W	Farming	KY
	M. R.	32	M	W		TN
	M. D. L.	25	M	W		TN
	Alvin	21	F	W		TN
	Alfred K.	20	M	W		TN
	Kisan	18	M	W		TN
	Amanda M.	16	F	W		TN
	Edward P. G.	13	M	W		TN
Christian,	James H.	29	M	W	Day Laborer	TN
	Elizabeth	24	F	W		KY
	William C.	8	M	W		TN
	James L.	6	M	W		TN
	Mira E.	4	F	W		TN
	Mitchel R.	9/12	M	W		TN
Price,	John	49	M	W	Farmer	KY
	Sarah	45	F	W		TN
	Pinina J.	21	F	W		TN
	Zilba A.	19	F	W		TN
	E. J.	18	M	W		TN
	Francis M.	16	M	W		TN
	Nancy A.	14	F	W		TN
	Benjamin	12	M	W		TN
	William L.	10	M	W		TN
	Lewis W.	7	M	W		TN
	Absolom N.	5	M	W		TN
	Farly C.	1	F	W		TN
Rains,	Mary A.	29	F	W	Tenant	TN
	Alvin C.	9	M	W		TN
	Henry Clay	6	M	W		TN
	Clarinda L.	3	F	W		TN
Paul,	Dan C.	25	M	W	Day Laborer	TN

1860 Fentress Co. TN Census

Name		Age Remarks	Sex	Race	Profession	Birth Place

Civil District No. 2
Recorded 14 June 1860

Name		Age	Sex	Race	Profession	Birth Place
Flowers,	J. P.	32	M	W	Farmer	KY
	Elizabeth	27	F	W		TN
	Charles P.	8	M	W		TN
	Lavina A. J.	7	F	W		TN
	Wiley R.	5	M	W		TN
	William J.	3	M	W		TN
	Arch Owens	1	M	W		TN
Mullinix,	Nathaniel	24	M	W	Tenant	TN
	Mary	19	F	W		TN
	Isham L.	1	M	W		TN
	Eli F.	21	M	W	Day Laborer	TN
	Andrew J.	17	M	W	Day Laborer	TN
Wood,	Jeremiah W.	30	M	W	Tenant	TN
	Jane	23	F	W		TN
	Alice C.	1	F	W		TN
Wood,	Mathew	60	M	W		NC
	Elizabeth	53	F	W		VA
	?	33	F	W		TN
	Jesse M.	25	M	W		TN
	George W.	23	M	W		TN
	Sarah A.	16	F	W		TN
	Charles C.	11	M	W		TN

Recorded 15 June 1860

Name		Age	Sex	Race	Profession	Birth Place
Wood,	Nancy	53	F	W	Farming	KY
	Elizabeth	31	F	W		TN
	Sarah A.	23	F	W		TN
	Jesse E.	21	M	W		TN
	Susanah J.	20	F	W		TN
	John B.	18	M	W		TN
	James S.	16	M	W		TN
	Anna C.	14	F	W		TN
	George W.	12	M	W		TN

1860 Fentress Co. TN Census

Name		Age Remarks	Sex	Race	Profession	Birth Place

Civil District No. 2
Recorded 15 June 1860

Name		Age	Sex	Race	Profession	Birth Place
Wood,	William H.	30	M	W	Farmer	TN
	Julia A. S.	17	F	W		KY
	Mary S.	1	F	W		KY
	Sarah E.	10 days	F	W		TN
Wood,	Jonathan	32	M	W	Farmer	TN
	Matilda	33	F	W		TN
	Franklin P.	7	M	W		TN
	Mary E.	3	F	W		TN
McClellon,	Lucinda	27	F	W	Domestic	TN
Taylor,	Isaac S.	25	M	W	Farmer	TN
Adkins,	James J.	63	M	W	Day Laborer	NC
	Mary	60	F	W		SC
	James M.	3	M	W		TN
Adkins,	George W.	43	M	W	Farmer	NC
	Mary	36	F	W		TN
	Eli	19	M	W		TN
	Winnie	15	F	W		TN
	Elizabeth	12	F	W		TN
	Serelda	8	F	W		TN
	Sherrod	7	M	W		TN
	Emma	5	F	W		TN
	David C.	3	M	W		TN
Smith,	Richard	39	M	W	Farmer	TN
	Nancy	40	F	W		TN
	David F.	13	M	W		TN
	Margaret L.	12	F	W		TN
	Philip J.	11	M	W		TN
	John L.	9	M	W		TN
	Sarah E.	7	F	W		TN
Conatser,	Lavina	53	F	W	Gardening	KY
Conatser,	William P.	26	M	W	Farmer	TN
	Jane	22	F	W		TN
	Melina E.	3	F	W		TN

1860 Fentress Co. TN Census

Name		Age Remarks	Sex	Race	Profession	Birth Place

Civil District No. 2
Recorded 15 June 1860

Name		Age	Sex	Race	Profession	Birth Place
Conatser,	John	39	M	W	Farmer	TN
	Elizabeth E.	25	F	W		TN
	Matilda J.	6	F	W		TN
	William P.	3	M	W		TN
	Margaret E.	2	F	W		TN
Woolsey,	George	37	M	W	Farmer	?
	Mary	73	F	W	Domestic	PA
	Anna	38	F	W		TN
	Sarah	28	F	W		TN
	Abigail	24	F	W		TN
Mathas,	Elisha	23	M	W	Day Laborer	IL
	Maranda L.	22	F	W		TN
	Joseph G.	11/12	M	W		TN
Greer,	Samuel	49	M	W	Minister MES	TN
	Jane	49	F	W		TN
	Mary	25	F	W		TN
	Benjamin F.	23	M	W	Farmer	TN
	Margaret	20	F	W		TN
	David	17	M	W		TN
Greer,	John C.	29	M	W	Tenant	TN
	Jane	28	F	W		TN
	Samuel Polk	7	M	W		TN
	Mary J.	3	F	W		TN
Robinson,	Enoch	66	M	W	Farmer	TN
	Elizabeth	56	F	W		TN
	Nancy J.	32	F	W		TN
	Sarah C.	26	F	W		TN
	Jesse L.	24	M	W		TN
	Alexander H.	22	M	W		TN
	Rachel W.	19	F	W		TN
	Obidiah	17	M	W		TN
	George G.	14	M	W		TN

1860 Fentress Co. TN Census

Name		Age Remarks	Sex	Race	Profession	Birth Place

Civil District No. 2
Recorded 15 June 1860

Name		Age	Sex	Race	Profession	Birth Place
Beaty,	John A.	32	M	W	Farmer	TN
	Mahala	35	F	W		TN
	Thomas	12	M	W		TN
	William	10	M	W		TN
	James R.	8	M	W		TN
	Green	6	M	W		TN
	Prince	4	M	W		TN
	Lewis	2	M	W		FN
	George	1/12	M	W		TN
Wood,	John B.	26	M	W	Physician	TN
	Marintha E.	21	F	W		KY
	Celeste M.	7/12	F	W		TN
Massingill,	Archabald	45	M	W	Day Laborer	TN
	Bethiah	21	F	W		TN
	M? J.	12	F	W		TN
	Mary C.	10	F	W		TN
	Nancy E.	7	F	W		TN
	John R.	6	M	W		TN
	Joseph A.	4	M	W		TN
	Rebeccah A.	2	F	W		TN
	Sarah A.	5/12	F	W		TN
Carney,	Nicholas	53	M	W	Day Laborer	VA
	Emeline	34	F	W		VA
	Patrick L.	14	M	W		TN
	William J.	12	M	W		TN
	Mathew	11	M	W		TN
	Margaret	8	F	W		TN
	John	6	M	W		TN
	Anna	5	F	W		TN
	Martin H.	3	M	W		TN
	S? V.	2/12	M	W		TN
Storie,	Oliver	23	M	W	Day Laborer	VA
	Rebeccah	19	F	W		TN
	John F.	1	M	W		TN

1860 Fentress Co. TN Census

Name		Age Remarks	Sex	Race	Profession	Birth Place

Civil District No. 2
Recorded 15 June 1860

Name		Age	Sex	Race	Profession	Birth Place
Storie,	William	27	M	W	Farmer	TN
	Anna	28	F	W		TN
	Joshua R.	5	M	W		TN
	Lewis Cass	3	M	W		TN
	Andrew J.	1	M	W		TN

Recorded 16 June 1860

Name		Age	Sex	Race	Profession	Birth Place
Storey,	N. W.	51	M	W	Farmer	NC
	Catharine	50	F	W		TN
	Sarah	24	F	W		TN
	Mary	21	F	W		TN
	John W.	19	M	W		TN
	Margaret	17	F	W		TN
	William F.	13	M	W		TN
	Catharine J.	11	F	W		TN
	Ephram	9	M	W		TN
Wood,	Jesse	50	M	W	Farmer	NC
	Matilda	48	F	W		TN
	Thomas G.	23	M	W		TN
	David H.	21	M	W		TN
	Mathew B.	19	M	W		TN
	William Y.	17	M	W		TN
	Pleasant B.	12	M	W		TN
	Mary J.	10	F	W		TN
	D. D.	5	M	W		TN
Mace,	Henry	75	M	W	Farmer	VA
	Lavina	75	F	W		VA
	Sarah J.	28	F	W		TN
Mace,	William C.	36	M	W	Tenant	TN
	Mary	20	F	W		KY
	Andrew J.	12	M	W		TN
	Lavina E.	2/12	F	W		TN
Mace,	Philip	40	M	W	Tenant	TN
	Mary A.	36	F	W		KY
	Alvin	2	M	W		TN
	William H. C.	6/12	M	W		TN

1860 Fentress Co. TN Census

Name		Age Remarks	Sex	Race	Profession	Birth Place	

Civil District No. 2
Recorded 16 June 1860

Name		Age	Sex	Race	Profession	Birth Place	
Reagan,	John	28	M	W	Tenant	TN	
	Melinda	21	F	W		TN	
	William	1	M	W		TN	
Carter,	Elizabeth	32	F	W	Tenant	TN	
	Eliza J.	16	F	W		TN	
	John W.	14	M	W		TN	
	George W.	10	M	W		TN	
	William B.	4	M	W		TN	
Bruce,	William	41	M	W	Farmer	TN	
	Mary	47	F	W		KY	
Holbert,	Stephen	50	M	W	Farmer	TN	
	Elizabeth	47	F	W		TN	
	Caroline	21	F	W		TN	
	Nathaniel	20	M	W	Tenant	TN	
	Joel	18	M	W		TN	
	Married within						
	Mary	17	F	W		TN	the
year							
	John	16	M	W		TN	
	Stephen	14	M	W		TN	
	Nancy A. E.	11	F	W		TN	
	Mary C.	7	F	W		TN	
	Jeremiah	4	M	W		TN	
Hinds,	Samuel	30	M	W	Farmer	TN	
	Alvina	27	F	W		KY	
	John I. A.	11	M	W		TN	
	Joel E.	10	M	W		TN	
	Margaret J.	7	F	W		TN	
	Nina A.	6	F	W		TN	
	Susanah M.	3	F	W		TN	
	Simon	4/12	M	W		TN	
Reagan,	Joel L.	53	M	W	Farmer	NC	
	Margaret	53	F	W		TN	
Pennycuff,	Archabald	23	M	W	Day Laborer	TN	
	Married within						
	Mahala	16	F	W		TN	the
year.							

1860 Fentress Co. TN Census

Name		Age Remarks	Sex	Race	Profession	Birth Place

Civil District No. 2
Recorded 16 June 1860

Name		Age	Sex	Race	Profession	Birth Place
Pennycuff,	Jacob	52	M	W		TN
	Elizabeth	26	F	W		TN
	Rachel	19	F	W		TN
	James	16	M	W		TN
	Mary J.	14	F	W		TN
	Nancy M.	5	F	W		TN
	John	3	M	W		TN
	David A.	1	M	W		FN
Pennycuff,	David	40	M	W	Farmer	TN
	Nancy J.	23	F	W		TN
	Elyiva	14	F	W		TN
	Joel	12	M	W		TN
	Mathew M. B.	9	M	W		TN
	William	7	M	W		TN
	John	4	M	W		TN
	Jacob F.	2	M	W		TN
	Elizabeth J.	7 days	F	W		TN

Recorded 19 June 1860

Name		Age	Sex	Race	Profession	Birth Place
Reagan,	Charles	57	M	W	Farmer	NC
	Levina	47	F	W		TN
	W. H.	20	M	W		TN
	James D.	19	M	W		TN
	Nancy J.	18	F	W		TN
	Jesse F.	16	M	W		TN
	George W.	14	M	W		TN
	Lavina	3	F	W		TN
Beaty,	John	26	M	W	Farmer	TN
	Zelpha	24	F	W		TN
	James G.	3	M	W		TN
	Margaret K.	2	F	W		TN

1860 Fentress Co. TN Census

Name		Age Remarks	Sex	Race	Profession	Birth Place

Civil District No. 2
Recorded 19 June 1860

Name		Age Remarks	Sex	Race	Profession	Birth Place
Mullinix,	Nathan	53	M	W	Tenant	TN
	Margaret	48	F	W		TN
	John	19	M	W		TN
	Nancy	14	F	W		TN
	N. A.	10	M	W		TN
	Margaret	6	F	W		TN
	Melinda	3	F	W		TN
Owens,	George	68	M	W	Tenant	TN
	Sarah	60	F	W		NC
	George W.	30	M	W		TN
	Jane	25	F	W		TN
	Charlotte	19	F	W		TN
	Samuel	22	M	W	Day Laborer	TN
Reagan,	John C.	29	M	W	Tenant	TN
	Rebecca	27	F	W		TN
	Elizabeth	6	F	W		TN
	John	4	M	W		TN
	Catharine	1	F	W		TN
Owen,	Thomas M.	27	M	W		TN
	Susanah	22	F	W		TN
	Samuel P.	1	M	W		TN
	John S.	7/12	M	W		TN
Reagan,	William	50	M	W	Farmer	TN
	Mary	46	F	W		TN
	Nancy	17	F	W		TN
	Joel	13	M	W		TN
	Catharine	4	F	W		TN
Choate,	Martha	24	F	W	Tenant	TN
	Anna	2	F	W		TN
	John	7 days	M	W		TN
	Ruth A.	16	F	W	Domestic	TN

1860 Fentress Co. TN Census

Name		Age Remarks	Sex	Race	Profession	Birth Place

Civil District No. 2
Recorded 19 June 1860

Name		Age	Sex	Race	Profession	Birth Place
Alred,	Thomas H.	29	M	W	Farmer	TN
	Mary A.	29	F	W		TN
	James A.	5	M	W		TN
	Lean	4/12	F	W		TN
Mathas,	Joseph	52	M	W	Farmer	NC
	Almira	45	F	W		NC
	John	20	M	W		KY
	Nancy	18	F	W		KY
	Rebeccah	18	F	W		KY
	Esther J.	16	F	W		IL
	Elijah	14	M	W		TN
	William	13	M	W		TN
	George W.	11	M	W		TN
	Hiram	9	M	W		TN
	Joseph D.	7	M	W		TN
	Jesse W.	6	M	W		TN
Mathas,	Thomas B.	29	M	W	Tenant	KY
	Mary	26	F	W		TN
	William W.	7	M	W		TN
	Sarah J.	4	F	W		TN
	Catharine M.	2	F	W		TN
Reagan,	Thomas	37	M	W	Farmer	TN
	Mary C.	27	F	W		KY
	William W.	4	M	W		TN
	Joseph L.	2	M	W		TN
	Joel L. H.	8/12	M	W		TN
Taylor,	John	65	M	W	Tenant	VA
	Anna	55	F	W		TN
	William J.	26	M	W	Saddler	TN
	John M.	20	M	W	Farming	TN
	Emmavilla	6	F	W		TN
Taylor,	James W. S.	36	M	W	Farmer	TN
	Nancy	30	F	W		TN
	Isaac F.	6	M	W		TN
	Susanah J.	3	F	W		TN
	John A.	1	M	W		TN

1860 Fentress Co. TN Census

Name		Age Remarks	Sex	Race	Profession	Birth Place

Civil District No. 2
Recorded 19 June 1860

Name		Age	Sex	Race	Profession	Birth Place
Wright,	Mathias	41	M	W		VA
	Elizabeth J.	43	F	W		VA
	James W.	19	M	W		TN
	Joseph H.	17	M	W		TN
	Margaret A.	15	F	W		TN
	Nancy	13	F	W		TN
	John T.	11	M	W		TN
	Jacob R.	9	M	W		FN
	Samuel	3	M	W		TN
	David M.	1	M	W		TN
Wright,	Mathew W.	72	M	W	Farmer	MD
	Margaret	70	F	W		VA
Wright,	David F.	32	M	W	Miller	TN
	Juda	32	F	W		TN
	Elizabeth P.	5	F	W		TN
	Martha A.	4	M	W		TN
	William S.	2	M	W		TN
	Moses L.	6/12	M	W		TN
Stringfield,	James	13	M	W		TN
Beaty,	Susan	58	F	W	Farming	NC
	James M.	24	M	W		TN
	Isaac R.	21	M	W		TN
	Lucy K.	19	F	W		TN
	David C.	15	M	W		TN
	Aley	12	M	W		TN
Beaty,	William R.	34	M	W	Farmer	TN
	Mary	28	F	W		TN
	Sarah	12	F	W		TN
	Susan	8	F	W		TN
	Isaac	7	M	W		TN
	Mary	5	F	W		TN
	Rebeccah	3	F	W		TN
	John	1	M	W		TN

1860 Fentress Co. TN Census

Name		Age Remarks	Sex	Race	Profession	Birth Place

Civil District No. 2
Recorded 19 June 1860

Name		Age Remarks	Sex	Race	Profession	Birth Place	
Adkins,	Eli H.	32	M	W	Farmer	TN	
	Nancy	33	F	W		TN	
	Edward	6	M	W		TN	
	George W.	5	M	W		TN	
	John A.	3	M	W		TN	
	Sarah A. E.	2	F	W		TN	

Recorded 20 June 1860

Name		Age Remarks	Sex	Race	Profession	Birth Place	
Lang,	Thomas	53	M	W	Farmer	Ireland	
	Eliza	45	F	W		Ireland	
	William H.	11	M	W		NY	
	Fanny	7	F	W		TN	
Gould,	John W.	53	M	W	Laborer Manufacturing	MD	
	Sarah W.	52	F	W		PA	
	Elizabeth C.	26	F	W		PA	
	Thomas W.	25	M	W		NY	
	Henry P.	21	M	W		MD	
	Hiser	15	M	W		NY	
	American	13	F	W		NY	
Albertson,	Soloman	50	M	W	Cooper	TN	
	Maria	46	F	W		TN	
	William E.	14	M	W		TN	
	Soloman	13	M	W		TN	
	Nicholas	11	M	W		TN	
	Milton L.	8	M	W		TN	
	Robert G.	4	M	W		TN	
	Mitchel	1	M	W		TN	
Culver,	John	66	M	W		TN	
	Nancy	50	F	W		NC	
	Stakely	19	M	W		TN	
	Thomas W.	16	M	W		TN	
	Lorenzo D.	14	M	W		TN	
	Ludema	13	F	W		TN	
	Jacob	10	M	W		TN	
Albertson,	Nancy J.	3	F	W		TN	
	Marzietta	1	F	W		TN	
Culver,	Susan	35	F	W	Domestic	TN	

1860 Fentress Co. TN Census

Name		Age Remarks	Sex	Race	Profession	Birth Place

Civil District No. 3
Recorded 20 June 1860

Name		Age Remarks	Sex	Race	Profession	Birth Place
Roark,	Bridget	50	F	W	Farming	Ireland
	Mary A.	15	F	W		NY
Albertson,	Soloman	36	M	W	Blacksmith	TN
	Emeline	36	F	W		KY
	Amanda E.	9	F	W		TN
	Mary A.	7	F	W		TN
	Thursa J.	1	F	W		TN
Hays,	Mary	39	F	W	Gardening	TN
	Mary J.	19	F	W		TN
	William J.	15	M	W	Laborer	TN
	F. M.	12	M	W		TN
	William E.	6	M	W		TN
	Henry C.	2	M	W		TN
	James E.	4	M	W		TN
	John	2	M	W		TN
	Unnamed	5/12	F	W		TN
Livingston,	Thomas E.	35	M	W	Blacksmith	TN
	Mary P.	37	F	W		KY
	Ambrose H.	9	M	W		KY
	Henry B.	7	M	W		KY
	Nancy J.	4	F	W		KY
	John M.	3	M	W		TN
	Lucetta A.	2	F	W		TN
Livingston,	Thomas	58	M	W	Farmer	KY
	Sarah	60	F	W		NC
	Celia	33	F	W		TN
	Melissa A.	25	F	W		TN
	David P.	22	M	W		TN
Northrup,	John I.	57	M	W	Farmer	NY
	Sybil B.	55	F	W		CT
Eppison,	Sarah	10	F	W		TN

1860 Fentress Co. TN Census

Name		Age Remarks	Sex	Race	Profession	Birth Place

Civil District No. 3
Recorded 20 June 1860

Name		Age	Sex	Race	Profession	Birth Place
Taylor,	Pleasant	49	M	W		TN
	Martha	47	F	W		TN
	Joseph C.	19	M	W		TN
	Diclama	17	F	W		TN
	Martha J.	12	F	W		TN
	Berry H.	9	M	W		TN
	Amanda	6	F	W		TN
	James P.	5	M	W		TN
	Isaac	76	M	W		TN
	Alfred	46	M	W		TN
McGee,	William J.	26	M	W	Farmer	TN
	Elizabeth M.	21	F	W		TN
	Kanzaida	1	F	W		TN
York,	Kenny M.	23	M	W	Farmer	TN
	Nancy J.	23	F	W		TN
Gallaway,	Elizabeth M.	64	F	W	Domestic	VA
Wright,	Jeremiah	46	M	W	Carpenter	TN
	Zibba	40	F	W		TN
	John R.	17	M	W	Day Laborer	TN
	Moses N.	14	M	W		TN
	Mary E.	11	F	W		TN
	Pevina C.	8	F	W		TN
	James M.	6	M	W		TN
	Martha E.	4	F	W		TN
Jackson,	James	72	M	W	Farmer	PA
	Andrew	22	M	W		OH
	Nancy J.	21	F	W		TN

Recorded 21 June 1860

Name		Age	Sex	Race	Profession	Birth Place
McGee,	William H.	62	M	W	Farmer Tenant	VA
	Sarah A.	60	F	W		KY

1860 Fentress Co. TN Census

Name		Age Remarks	Sex	Race	Profession	Birth Place

Civil District No. 3
Recorded 21 June 1860

Name		Age	Sex	Race	Profession	Birth Place
McGee,	Joel L.	34	M	W	Farmer	TN
	Mary A.	22	F	W		
	John T.	3	M	W		
	William F.	1	M	W		
	Tranquilla	1/12	F	W		TN
Rich,	Landon	11	M	W		TN
Philips,	Abner	58	M	W	Farmer	KY
	Bula A.	49	F	W		KY
	Joseph C.	25	M	W		TN
	McKayer R.	21		W		TN
	Pleasant L.	17	F	W		TN
	Nancy E.	15	F	W		TN
	Benjamin H.	12	M	W		TN
	Hiram A.	6	M	W		TN
White,	James	31	M	W	Day Laborer	Ireland
Gatewood,	Pembleton	54	M	W	Farmer Tenant	KY
	Nancy	52	F	W		KY
	J. Henry	26	M	W		KY
	Berry	20	M	W		TN
	Milton L.	16	M	W		TN
	John	12	M	W		TN
	Mary	10	F	W		TN
	Sarah F.	8	F	W		TN
	Abner L.	5	M	W		TN
Moat,	Thomas	49	M	W		Ireland
	Esther	49	F	W		NJ
	William S.	19	M	W		PA
	Oswell J.	17	M	W		PA
	Elizabeth	14	F	W		PA
	Mary	10	F	W		PA
	James	9	M	W		PA
	Mary	79	F	W	Domestic	PA

1860 Fentress Co. TN Census

Name		Age Remarks	Sex	Race	Profession	Birth Place

Civil District No. 3
Recorded 21 June 1860

Name		Age	Sex	Race	Profession	Birth Place
McGee,	James L.	28	M	W	Farmer Tenant	TN
	Inglintein	25	F	W		TN
	Lucienna	5	F	W		TN
	Travis	3	M	W		TN
	Claranza J.	1	F	W		TN
Lavender,	Jefferson	39	M	W	Farmer	TN
	Rebeccah A.	25	F	W		KY
	Martha	6	F	W		TN
	Milly J.	4	F	W		TN
	Sarah M.	1	F	W		TN
Bales,	Robert	62	M	W	Farmer	TN
	Jane	56	F	W		KY
	James	28	M	W		TN
	Martha	25	F	W		TN
	Emeline	19	F	W		TN
	George R.	16	M	W		TN
	Alexander	15	M	W		TN
	Vienna	10	F	W		TN
Simpson,	Job	56	M	W	Farmer	OH
	Jane	52	F	W		NC
	Elizabeth J.	19	F	W		TN
	Balaam	17	M	W		TN
	William	14	M	W		TN
	Martha	11	F	W		TN
Scott,	George	58	M	W	Carpenter	PA
Hirndon,	R. P.	51	M	W		KY
	Rebeccah	35	F	W		TN
	E. L.	16	?	W		KY
	Sarah C.	12	F	W		TN
	Susan M.	9	F	W		TN
	William C.	7	M	W		TN
	Thomas P. D.	4	M	W		TN
	Mildred J.	2	F	W		TN

1860 Fentress Co. TN Census

Name		Age	Sex	Race	Profession	Birth Place
		Remarks				

Civil District No. 3
Recorded 21 June 1860

Name		Age	Sex	Race	Profession	Birth Place
Williams,	Alfred	35	M	W	Farmer	TN
	Philip	26	M	W		TN
	Mary	21	F	W		TN
Bledsoe,	A.	30	M	W	Atty. at Law	KY
	Elizabeth F.	19	F	W		KY
	Lilian B.	1	F	W		TN
	Owen John	9	M	W		KY
Cummings,	Mary	22	F	W	Domestic	KY
Hurst,	Robert	34	M	W	Farmer	TN
	Cinthia	32	F	W		TN
	Emma	12	F	W		TN
	Millard F.	7	M	W		TN
	Lewis C.	6	M	W		TN
	John C.	4	M	W		TN
	Francis M.	1	M	W		TN
	Genetta	26	F	W	Domestic	TN
	Oliver	23	M	W	Day Laborer	TN
Kuckendoffer,	R. H.	45	M	W	Tanner	KY
	Elizabeth	31	F	W		KY
	H. C.	12	M	W		KY
	M. S.	5	F	W		KY
	C. S.	4	M	W		KY
	D. A.	2	M	W		KY
Collins,	Jasper	21	M	W	Apprentice Tanner	KY
Baily,	William	61	M	W	Carpenter	Ireland
Brown,	Robert	43	M	W	Cabinet Workman	TN
	Louisa	34	F	W		NC
	Sarah	18	F	W		TN
	Luanna	16	F	W		TN
	Joel	13	M	W		TN
	John M.	11	M	W		TN
	Elijah L.	9	M	W		TN
	Phebe	6	F	W		TN
	Fremont	2	M	W		TN

1860 Fentress Co. TN Census

Name		Age Remarks	Sex	Race	Profession	Birth Place

Civil District No. 3
Recorded 21 June 1860

Name		Age	Sex	Race	Profession	Birth Place
Crabtree,	Hiram	50	M	W	Farmer	KY
	Eda	47	F	W		TN
	Clarborne	19	M	W		TN
	G?	16	F	W		TN
	Eveline	14	F	W		TN
	Bailar	11	M	W		TN
	James	7	M	W		TN
	Manerva J.	5	F	W		TN
Delk,	Sherrd	35	M	W	Blacksmith	TN
	Melissa	28	F	W		TN
	Zerelda	12	F	W		TN
	Martha A.	8	F	W		TN
	Pleasant	6	M	W		TN
	David	7/12	M	W		TN

Recorded 22 June 1860

Name		Age	Sex	Race	Profession	Birth Place
Hall,	Thomas	30	M	W	Day Laborer	KY
	Mary	22	F	W		KY
	Martha A.	8	F	W		KY
	Cinthia C.	6	F	W		KY
	Mary M.	3	F	W		KY
Simpson,	James H.	37	M	W	Farmer	TN
	Martha T.	28	F	W		TN
	R. P.	10	M	W		TN
	F. P.	7	M	W		TN
	Francis M.	5	M	W		TN
	John W.	3	M	W		TN
	Mary E.	1	F	W		TN
Pague,	Soloman	44	M	W	Farming	TN
	Niza J.	31	F	W		TN
	Hiram F.	1/12	M	W		TN

1860 Fentress Co. TN Census

Name		Age Remarks	Sex	Race	Profession	Birth Place

Civil District No. 3
Recorded 22 June 1860

Name		Age	Sex	Race	Profession	Birth Place
Smith,	Charles	55	M	W	Farmer Tenant	TN
	Elizabeth	47	F	W		TN
	Mary	19	F	W		TN
	Sarah	16	F	W		TN
	Inglintine	13	F	W		TN
	David	10	M	W		TN
	Amanda J.	6	F	W		TN
Wright,	Masis	64	M	W	Farmer	GA
	Nancy	60	F	W		VA
Pluckett,	Conrad	35	M	W	Farmer	TN
	Mary	28	F	W		KY
	William R.	8	M	W		TN
	James	6	M	W		TN
	Sidna	5	F	W		TN
	Malvina	5	F	W		TN
	Calvin	2	M	W		TN
Crockett,	Dililah	70	F	W	Domestic	NC
Crockett,	William N.	32	M	W	Farmer Tenant	TN
	Rebeccah	30	F	W		TN
	Lucinda	7	F	W		TN
	Granville	3	M	W		TN
	Robert	11/12	M	W		TN
Smith,	Jeremiah	11	M	W		TN
Smith,	David	26	M	W	Farmer	TN
	Mary	26	F	W		TN
	William	8	M	W		TN
Stepp,	John	51	M	W	Farmer	NC
	Amanda	33	F	W		TN
	Mary	15	F	W		KY
	William	12	M	W		KY
	James	10	M	W		TN
	Catharine	8	M	W		TN
	Elizabeth	6	F	W		TN
	John	3	M	W		TN
	Preston	5/12	M	W		TN
Hicks,	Mary	64	F	W	Domestic	NC

1860 Fentress Co. TN Census

Name		Age Remarks	Sex	Race	Profession	Birth Place

Civil District No. 3
Recorded 22 June 1860

Name		Age	Sex	Race	Profession	Birth Place
Paul,	Samuel	34	M	W	Farmer	VA
	Elizabeth	25	F	W		TN
	Sarah J.	11	F	W		TN
	Alexander	7	M	W		TN
	John	4	M	W		TN
Caleb,	Thomas	41	M	W	Farmer	TN
	Sarah	41	F	W		TN
	Dililah F.	19	F	W		TN
	Abigail	18	F	W		TN
	William	16	M	W		TN
	John	12	M	W		TN
	Genetta	8	F	W		TN
	Elijada	2	F	W		TN
Wright,	Thomas	58	M	W	Farmer	VA
	Lydia	50	F	W		TN
	Smith W.	14	M	W		TN
	Amilia M.	11	F	W		KY
	Clayton T.	8	M	W		TN
	Alexander	5	M	W		TN
Whit?,	Albert	60	M	W	Day Laborer	NC
	Lucy	65	F	W		NC
	Elizabeth	27	F	W		TN
	Albert	22	M	W	Day Laborer	TN
	James	25	M	W		TN
Owens,	Benjamin D.	26	M	W	Physician	KY
	America C.	20	F	W		KY
	Allison	5/12	M	W		KY
Whitenburg,	William	54	M	W	Farmer Tenant	TN
	Mary A.	34	F	W		TN
	Hiram	16	M	W		TN
	Elizabeth	14	F	W		TN
	Magnetta	10	F	W		TN
	Mary J.	7	F	W		TN
	Ordelia	6	F	W		TN
	James M.	4	M	W		TN
	Henry N.	2	M	W		TN
	William C.	6/12	M	W		TN

46

1860 Fentress Co. TN Census

Name		Age Remarks	Sex	Race	Profession	Birth Place

Civil District No. 4
Recorded 25 June 1860

Name		Age	Sex	Race	Profession	Birth Place
Bowdon,	Joshua S.	32	M	W	Farmer	TN
	Mary A.	28	F	W		TN
	Drucilla	9	F	W		TN
	Susan	7	F	W		TN
	Granville H.	3	M	W		TN
	Charlotte H.	1	F	W		TN
Choate,	Thomas	53	M	W	Farmer	NC
	Mary	50	F	W		TN
	Austin	23	M	W	Farmer	TN
	Louisa	18	F	W		TN
	Sabe	16	M	W	Farmer	TN
	Amanda	13	F	W		TN
	George	11	M	W		TN
	Benjamin	5	M	W		TN
	John	25	M	W	Tenant	TN
Franklin,	Jackson	26	M	W	Tenant	TN
	Matilda	28	F	W		TN
	Mary	4/12	F	W		TN
Moody,	Peter	38	M	W	Farmer	TN
	Nancy	36	F	W		TN
	John	15	M	W	Farmer	TN
	Margaret	12	F	W		TN
	Nancy	8	F	W		TN
	James	5	M	W		TN
	Catharine	3	F	W		TN
	Benjamin	1	M	W		TN
Choate,	Gabrail	44	M	W	Day Laborer	TN
	Melinda	40	F	W		TN
	Margaret	23	F	W		TN
	Nancy	17	F	W		TN
	Elizabeth	15	F	W		TN
	Dililah	13	F	W		TN
	Samuel	10	M	W		TN
	Sarah	7	F	W		TN
	Mary	4	F	W		TN

1860 Fentress Co. TN Census

Name		Age Remarks	Sex	Race	Profession	Birth Place

Civil District No. 4
Recorded 25 June 1860

Name		Age	Sex	Race	Profession	Birth Place
Moody,	Jonathan	21	M	W	Farmer	TN
	Charlotte	18	F	W		TN
	Nancy J.	1	F	W		TN
Stephens,	A. J.	30	M	W	Farmer	TN
	Charlotte	29	F	W		TN
	William H. S.	9	M	W		TN
	Manson	8	M	W		TN
	Lydia	4	F	W		TN
	Matilda J.	2	F	W		TN
	Reese H.	5/12	M	W		TN
	Thomas J.	15	M	W	Day Laborer	TN
Stephens,	Burton	37	M	W	Farmer	TN
	Elizabeth	35	F	W		TN
	John F.	15	M	W	Farmer	TN
	George	13	M	W		TN
	James J.	10	M	W		TN
	Zilpha	8	F	W		TN
	Ava	4	F	W		TN
	William	3	M	W		TN
	Artilla	1	F	W		TN
Owens,	John	45	M	W	Tenant	TN
	Susan	40	F	W		TN
	Martin V.	20	M	W	Tenant	TN
	James	17	M	W	Tenant	TN
	Thomas	14	M	W		TN
	Lonengo D.	13	M	W		TN
	Miza	12	F	W		TN
	Joseph F.	8	M	W		TN
	William H.	6	M	W		TN
	Mary J.	1	F	W		TN
Stephens,	B. L.	21	M	W	Farmer	TN
	Charlotte J.	24	F	W		KY
	Hannah B.	1	F	W		TN
	Nisa A.	45	F	W	Domestic	TN
Sumptes?,	John P.	20	M	W	Tenant	KY

1860 Fentress Co. TN Census

Name		Age Remarks	Sex	Race	Profession	Birth Place

Civil District No. 4
Recorded 25 June 1860

Name		Age	Sex	Race	Profession	Birth Place
Cole,	Spencer M.	25	M	W	Farmer	TN
	Anna	25	F	W		KY
	Gesatta	2	F	W		TN
	John E.	1	M	W		TN
	Martha	52	F	W	Domestic	TN
Owens,	Mary	90	F	W	Domestic	NC

Recorded 26 June 1860

Name		Age	Sex	Race	Profession	Birth Place
Fulton,	David	29	M	W	Day Laborer	TN
	Tabitha C.	25	F	W		TN
	Catharine E.	3	F	W		TN
	William R.	1	M	W		TN
Stephens,	Lydia	40	F	W	Laboring	TN
	Fanny	5	F	W		TN
Cable,	Samuel	29	M	W	Farmer	TN
	Catharine	29	F	W		TN
	Mary E.	4	F	W		TN
	Nancy J.	3	F	W		TN
	Fanny E.	4/12	F	W		TN
Conatser,	David	52	M	W	Farmer Tenant	TN
	Geratta	50	F	W		TN
	Sarah	24	F	W		TN
	Mary	22	F	W		TN
	George	19	M	W	Farmer	TN
	Andrew	16	M	W		TN
	Abram	14	M	W		TN
	James	12	M	W		TN
	David	10	M	W		TN
Wood,	Thomas	30	M	W	Farmer	TN
	Rachel	30	F	W		VA
	Sarah E.	6	F	W		TN
	John W.	3	M	W		TN
	Jeremiah	10/12	M	W		TN

1860 Fentress Co. TN Census

Name		Age Remarks	Sex	Race	Profession	Birth Place

Civil District No. 4
Recorded 26 June 1860

Name		Age	Sex	Race	Profession	Birth Place
Hogue,	Soloman	25	M	W	Farmer	TN
	Caroline	20	F	W		TN
	John H.	3	M	W		TN
	Catherine	1	F	W		TN
Hogue,	Milburn	55	M	W	Farmer	KY
	Rachel	49	F	W		TN
	Pleasant	10	M	W		TN
	Elizabeth	66	F	W	Domestic	KY
Hogue,	Anthony	21	M	W	Tenant	TN
	Agnes	17	F	W		TN
York,	William	32	M	W	Farmer	TN
	Elizabeth	21	F	W		TN
	Andrew J.	6	M	W		TN
	Mary A.	4	F	W		TN
	Samuel G.	2	M	W		TN
	Latan R.	1	M	W		TN
Stephens,	John	29	M	W	Tenant	TN
	Eliza A.	31	F	W		TN
	Franklin P.	5	M	W		TN
	Jesse	3	M	W		TN
	Samantha J.	1	F	W		TN
	Isiah	20	M	W	Day Laborer	TN
York,	Jesse R.	53	M	W	Farmer	NC
	Melinda	52	F	W		GA
	Charlotte	22	F	W		TN
	Melinda C.	19	F	W		TN
	George	15	M	W		TN
	Balaam L.	12	M	W		TN
	Leiberca?	11	F	W		TN
	Sarah E.	7	F	W		TN
Wood,	Zephamiah	26	M	W	Tenant	TN
	Rachel	25	F	W		TN
	Melinda	6	F	W		TN
	Sarah A.	4	F	W		TN
	Helen R. J.	1	F	W		TN

50

1860 Fentress Co. TN Census

Name		Age Remarks	Sex	Race	Profession	Birth Place	

Civil District No. 4
Recorded 26 June 1860

Name		Age	Sex	Race	Profession	Birth Place	Remarks
Wood,	Elijah	50	M	W	Farmer	TN	
	Sarah	45	F	W		TN	
	Jeremiah	32	M	W		TN	
	Soloman	25	M	W		TN	
	Louisa	18	F	W		TN	
	Elizabeth	16	F	W		TN	
Wood,	John	23	M	W	Tenant	TN	
	Nancy	23	F	W		TN	
York,	Jefferson	47	M	W	Tenant	TN	
	Rhoda	30	F	W		KY	
	Lucy A.	18	F	W		TN	Idiotic
	Mathew	16	M	W		TN	
	William R.	4	M	W		TN	
	Philip C.	2	M	W		TN	
	Jefferson G.	11/12	M	W		TN	
Alred,	Lewis	25	M	W	Farmer	TN	
	Ellen	26	F	W		TN	
	Elizabeth	58	F	W	Domestic	NC	
	Elizabeth	14	F	W	Domestic	TN	

Recorded 27 June 1860

Name		Age	Sex	Race	Profession	Birth Place	Remarks
Stephens,	Russell	40	M	W	Farmer	TN	
	Catharine	32	F	W		TN	
	David	14	M	W		TN	
	Marion	12	M	W		TN	
	Eliza J.	10	F	W		TN	
	Edward	7	M	W		TN	
	John	3	M	W		TN	
	Cable	1	M	W		TN	
Griden,	Jesse	30	M	W	Farmer	TN	
	Elander	29	F	W		TN	
	Jane	4	F	W		TN	
	William P.	2	M	W		TN	
	Matilda E.	15 days	F	W		TN	

1860 Fentress Co. TN Census

Name		Age Remarks	Sex	Race	Profession	Birth Place

Civil District No. 4
Recorded 27 June 1860

Name		Age	Sex	Race	Profession	Birth Place
Franklin,	Clark	56	M	W	Tailor	TN
	Mary	36	F	W		TN
	Elias	11	M	W		TN
	Jesse	6	M	W		TN
	Margaret	5	F	W		TN
	Milley	3	F	W		TN
	Leura	4/12	F	W		TN
Richards,	John	35	M	W	Farmer	KY
	Nancy J.	26	F	W		TN
	Sarah J.	8	F	W		KY
	Barbara A.	5	F	W		TN
	Mary A.	4	F	W		TN
	Nancy E.	2	F	W		TN
	Laura B.	1	F	W		TN
Boles,	Robert F.	31	M	W	Tenant	TN
	Naoma	31	F	W		TN
	John	8	M	W		TN
	Alexander	5	M	W		TN
	James B.	3	M	W		TN
	George	1	M	W		TN
Reagan,	John	57	M	W	Farmer	NC
	Nancy	43	F	W		TN
	Joel L.	19	M	W	Farmer	TN
	William L.	17	M	W	Farmer	TN
	James M. P.	14	M	W		TN
	Thomas J.	12	M	W		TN
	John	11	M	W		TN
	Mardaret J.	9	F	W		TN
	Andrew	7	M	W		TN
	Martha	4	F	W		TN
Winningham,	John	34	M	W	Farmer	TN
	Nancy	27	F	W		TN
Stephens,	Rebeccah	16	F	W	Domestic	TN
	Thomas	17	M	W	Day Laborer	TN
Hoover,	Samuel	27	M	W	Tenant	TN
	Lucetta	21	F	W		TN

1860 Fentress Co. TN Census

Name		Age Remarks	Sex	Race	Profession	Birth Place

Civil District No. 4
Recorded 27 June 1860

Name		Age	Sex	Race	Profession	Birth Place
Stephens,	Miles	41	M	W	Tenant	TN
	Luvana	37	F	W		TN
	Mitchel	16	M	W		TN
	William	13	M	W		TN
	Lewis	11	M	W		TN
	George M.	4	M	W		TN
	Arminta	1	F	W		TN
	Anna	72	F	W	Domestic	SC
Stephens,	Zorababel	42	M	W	Tenant	TN
	Sarah	43	F	W		TN
	John	20	M	W	Tenant	TN
	David	17	M	W	Tenant	TN
	James	15	M	W	Tenant	TN
	Anna	11	F	W		TN
	Alexander	9	M	W		TN
	Thomas	6	M	W		TN
	Burton	4	M	W		TN
Ledbetter,	Hetty	43	F	W	Tenant	TN
	William B.	16	M	W		TN
Owens,	Nancy A.	49	F	W	Tenant	AL
Gunter,	Pleasant C.	18	M	W	Laborer	TN

Recorded 28 June 1860

Name		Age	Sex	Race	Profession	Birth Place
Abston,	Francis	54	M	W	Blacksmith	VA
	Mary J.	35	F	W		KY
	James D.	18	M	W	Farming	KY
	Sophia	16	F	W		MD
	Clementine	9	F	W		KY
	Joshua	7	M	W		KY
	Stephen	5	M	W		KY
	Catharine	1	F	W		TN
Page,	William	23	M	W	Tenant	KY
	Mary A.	21	F	W		KY
	Elizabeth J.	2	F	W		KY

1860 Fentress Co. TN Census

Name		Age Remarks	Sex	Race	Profession	Birth Place

Civil District No. 4
Recorded 28 June 1860

Name		Age	Sex	Race	Profession	Birth Place	
Riddle,	Isaac	60	M	W	Farmer	VA	
	Catharine	57	F	W		TN	
	Elizabeth	15	F	W		TN	
York,	Isaac	9	M	W		TN	
	Catharine	7	F	W		TN	
Abston,	Thomas	24	M	W	Tenant	TN	
	Married within						
	Happy F.	19	F	W		TN	the
year							
Riddle,	Joseph J.	34	M	W	Farmer	KY	
	Nancy	30	F	W		TN	
	Sarah	9	F	W		TN	
	Catharine	7	F	W		TN	
	Gaither	4	M	W		TN	
	Isaac F.	9/12	M	W		TN	
Balwin,	Wesley	49	M	W	Farmer	NC	
	Elizabeth	45	F	W		IL	
	Nancy A.	20	F	W		TN	
	William H.	19	M	W	Farmer	TN	
	John C.	16	M	W	Farmer	TN	
	Wiatt	15	M	W	Farmer	TN	
	Malvina	14	F	W		TN	
	Lafayette	11	M	W		TN	
	Eliza J.	9	F	W		TN	
	Robert W.	3	M	W		TN	
Ashburn,	E. M.	27	M	W	Farmer	TN	
	Milly	21	F	W		TN	
	Martha J.	5	F	W		TN	
	Jesse	3	M	W		TN	
	Robert W.	2	M	W		TN	
	William A.	4/12	M	W		TN	
Cook,	William	35	M	W	Farmer	TN	
	Nancy D.	28	F	W		TN	
	Mary A. E.	8	F	W		TN	
	Ruben P.	5	M	W		TN	
	George W.	3	M	W		TN	
	Jesse H.	5/12	M	W		TN	
	Jackson	12	M	W		TN	

1860 Fentress Co. TN Census

Name		Age Remarks	Sex	Race	Profession	Birth Place	

Civil District No. 4
Recorded 28 June 1860

Name		Age	Sex	Race	Profession	Birth Place	
Davis	Nelson	52	M	W	Tenant	KY	
	Elizabeth	44	F	W		TN	
	John	18	M	W	Tenant	TN	
	Mary	16	F	W		TN	
	Elizabeth	15	F	W		TN	
	Nancy	14	F	W		TN	
	William	12	M	W		TN	
	Francis M.	11	M	W		TN	
	Christian	9	F	W		TN	
	Lewis N.	8	M	W		TN	
	Margaret	3	F	W		TN	
Cook,	John	73	M	W	Farmer	VA	
	Sarah	56	F	W		NC	
	John J.	21	M	W		TN	
	Nathan T.	10	M	W		TN	
Ashburn,	Robert	48	M	W	Farmer	TN	
	Hetty	24	F	W		TN	
	James A.	22	M	W		TN	
	Ellison	17	M	W		TN	
	Lucinda	15	F	W		TN	Deaf &
Dumb							
	Armilda	14	F	W		TN	
	Jesse	11	M	W		TN	
	William H.	5	M	W		TN	
	John T.	2	M	W		TN	
	Unnamed	4/12	M	W		TN	
Neilly,	Robert	45	M	W	Blacksmith	VA	
	Susan M.	47	F	W		VA	
	Mary V.	16	F	W		VA	
	Jessmia J.	14	F	W		VA	
	Samuel W.	12	M	W		VA	
	Hugh A.	11	M	W		TN	
	James C.	8	M	W		TN	
	Martha A.	5	F	W		TN	
	Bates C.	3	M	W		TN	

1860 Fentress Co. TN Census

Name		Age Remarks	Sex	Race	Profession	Birth Place

Civil District No. 4
Recorded 28 June 1860

Name		Age	Sex	Race	Profession	Birth Place
Key,	Stephen	34	M	W	Farmer	TN
	Matilda	35	F	W		TN
	William A.	9	M	W		TN
	Nancy J.	7	F	W		TN
	Mary C.	5	F	W		TN
	Elander C.	2	F	W		TN
Cook,	William	65	M	W	Tenant	TN
	Jane	54	F	W		KY
	Andrew J.	23	M	W		TN
	Mary A.	8	F	W		TN
Whited,	William	50	M	W	Farmer	TN
	Lucinda	48	F	W		TN
	Alexander	23	M	W		TN
	Elizabeth	20	F	W		TN
	Martha A.	18	F	W		IL
	James	15	M	W		TN
	William B.	1	M	W		TN
Ashburn,	Jesse	70	M	W	Farmer	TN
	Martha	75	F	W		VA
Ashburn,	G. D.	31	M	W	Farmer	TN
	Lutitia	34	F	W		TN
	Anderson	12	M	W		TN
	Robert W.	10	M	W		TN
	Martha A.	8	F	W		TN
	Sarah J.	4	F	W		TN
	John H.	2	M	W		TN

Recorded 29 June 1860

Name		Age	Sex	Race	Profession	Birth Place
Stanton,	Leroy	46	M	W	Farmer	TN
	Genitta	22	F	W		TN
	F. M.	18	M	W		TN
	Parlee	16	F	W		TN
	Andrew J.	15	M	W		TN
	Agnes	12	F	W		TN
	Mahala J.	7	F	W		TN

1860 Fentress Co. TN Census

Name		Age Remarks	Sex	Race	Profession	Birth Place

Civil District No. 4
Recorded 29 June 1860

Name		Age	Sex	Race	Profession	Birth Place
Langford,	J. Wesley	36	M	W	Farmer	TN
	Eliza E.	40	F	W		TN
	Thomas N.	14	M	W		TN
	John H.	12	M	W		TN
	Sarah J.	11	F	W		TN
	William H.	8	M	W		TN
	James A.	7	M	W		TN
	George A.	6	M	W		TN
	Stephen H. C.	2	M	W		TN
Pennycuff,	Mathew	36	M	W	Tenant	TN
	Elander	34	F	W		TN
	Jane	18	F	W		TN
	Elizabeth	15	F	W		TN
	James	13	M	W		TN
	John	12	M	W		TN
	Margaret	9	F	W		TN
	Lawnay?	6	M	W		TN
	William	3	M	W		TN
	Amanda M.	1	F	W		TN
Padgett,	Jonathan	32	M	W	Tenant	TN
	Margaret	36	F	W		TN
	Carroll	8	M	W		TN
	Elizabeth	7	F	W		TN
	John	6	M	W		TN
	Andrew J.	4	M	W		TN
	William	2	M	W		TN
	Martha J.	1	F	W		TN
Bledson,	E. B.	38	M	W	Farmer	KY
	Mary E.	27	F	W		TN
	William H.	8	M	W		TN
	Elizabeth V.	6	F	W		TN
	Robert B.	4	M	W		TN
	William M.	68	M	W	Farmer	KY
	Elizabeth	60	F	W		NC

1860 Fentress Co. TN Census

Name		Age Remarks	Sex	Race	Profession	Birth Place

Civil District No. 4
Recorded 29 June 1860

Name		Age	Sex	Race	Profession	Birth Place
Wright,	Joshua	83	M	W	Farmer	NC
	Sarah	77	F	W		NC
Deweese?,	John	61	M	W	Farmer	VA
	Sarah	62	F	W		VA
Adkins,	Jesse	72	M	W	Tenant	TN
	Sarah	70	F	W		VA
Franklin,	Malvina	28	F	W	Domestic	TN
	Martha J.	8	F	W		TN
	William J.	7	M	W		TN
	Jesse A.	6	M	W		TN
	Isaac N.	4	M	W		TN
	Wiatt A.	3	M	W		TN
Lee,	Margaret M.	9	F	W		TN
Gowney,	Banks	36	M	W	Wagoner	TN
	Margaret	35	F	W		TN
	Timothy	13	M	W		TN
	Mary	12	F	W		TN
	William	8	M	W		TN
	Elizabeth J.	7	F	W		TN
	Eliza A.	5	F	W		TN
	John	2	M	W		TN
Bowdon,	William B.	34	M	W	Farmer	TN
	Sarah	29	F	W		KY
	Razetta	10	F	W		TN
	Landon V.	9	M	W		TN
	Elas F.	7	M	W		TN
	John W.	5	M	W		TN
	Guinn V.	3	M	W		TN
	Sainnds? N.	6/12	M	W		TN
Young,	Rebeccah J.	21	F	W		TN
Franklin,	Nathaniel	21	M	W	Day Laborer	IN
	Caroline	18	F	W		TN
	Jesse	1	M	W		TN
	Nancy J.	5/12	F	W		TN

1860 Fentress Co. TN Census

Name		Age Remarks	Sex	Race	Profession	Birth Place

Civil District No. 4
Recorded 29 June 1860

Name		Age	Sex	Race	Profession	Birth Place
Beaty,	William C.	35	M	W	Farmer	TN
	Emeline	30	F	W		TN
	Matilda	12	F	W		TN
	Martha J.	10	F	W		TN
	John M.	8	M	W		TN
	James M.	6	M	W		TN
	Mary A.	3	F	W		TN
Stephens,	Gemn?	45	M	W	Farmer	TN
	Milley	36	F	W		TN
	Mary	12	F	W		TN
	Rufus S.	11	M	W		TN
	Balaam L.	9	M	W		TN
	E. S.	7	M	W		TN
	Cobb C.	5	M	W		TN
	William J.	3	M	W		TN
	Hosia B.	1	M	W		TN
Turner,	Nathan	54	M	W	Farmer	SC
	Delilah	38	F	W		TN
	Nancy	16	F	W		TN
	Sarah	12	F	W		TN
	Rachel	8	F	W		TN
	Mary	5	F	W		TN
	Gen P.	3	M	W		TN
	Tanzy	2	F	W		TN
Young,	Leander	23	M	W	Farmer	TN
	Nisa	19	F	W		TN
	Milly J.	1	F	W		TN
Turner,	James	63	M	W	Farmer	SC
	Nisa A.	62	F	W		VA
Young,	James	25	M	W	Farmer	TN
	Melissa	23	F	W		TN
	John	2	M	W		TN
	Hugh R.	1	M	W		TN

1860 Fentress Co. TN Census

Name		Age Remarks	Sex	Race	Profession	Birth Place

Civil District No. 4
Recorded 29 June 1860

Name		Age	Sex	Race	Profession	Birth Place
Beaty,	John	45	M	W	Farmer	TN
	Narsissa	40	F	W		TN
	Joel	20	M	W		TN
York,	Greenville	6	M	W		TN

Recorded 30 June 1860

Name		Age	Sex	Race	Profession	Birth Place
Stephens,	Edward	28	M	W	Farmer	TN
	Elizabeth	25	F	W		TN
	Mary A.	1	F	W		TN
	David	30	M	W		TN
York,	Mriah	35	M	W	Farmer	TN
	Eliza	30	F	W		TN
	Calia	4	F	W		TN
	John H.	2	M	W		TN
McGee,	Robert C.	22	M	W	Farmer	TN
	Catharine	19	F	W		TN
	Mary E.	1	F	W		TN

1860 Fentress Co. TN Census

Name		Age Remarks	Sex	Race	Profession	Birth Place

Civil District No. 5
Recorded 23 July 1860

Name		Age	Sex	Race	Profession	Birth Place
Crabtree,	Samuel	61	M	W	Blacksmith	VA
	Josie	35	F	W		TN
	Louisa	14	F	W		TN
	John W. M.	12	M	W		TN
	Wisam	9	M	W		TN
	Nimrod	6	M	W		TN
	Levina	4	F	W		TN
	Burdoin	3	M	W		TN
	Moses	11/12	M	W		TN
Seston?,	Aaron	34	M	W	Farmer	TN
	Nancy	31	F	W		KY
	John	11	M	W		TN
	Julia	9	M	W		TN
	Amanda	6	F	W		TN
	Menford	3	M	W		TN
	Pirsy	10/12	M	W		TN
Doss,	William D.	26	M	W	Farmer	TN
	Nancy	23	F	W		TN
	Joseph C.	3/12	M	W		TN
Crabtree,	Isaac	35	M	W	Farmer	TN
	Sarah	29	F	W		TN
	Samuel	29	M	W		TN
	Nancy E.	9	F	W		TN
	Mary J.	6	F	W		TN
	Hiram	5	M	W		TN
	Selina M.	2	F	W		TN
Alexander,	William	24	M	W	Farmer	KY
	Mary	39	F	W		KY
	Diancy	5	F	W		KY
	Lucinda	4	F	W		KY
	Miley	3	F	W		KY
	Agers	9/12	M	W		KY

1860 Fentress Co. TN Census

Name		Age Remarks	Sex	Race	Profession	Birth Place

Civil District No. 5
Recorded 23 July 1860

Name		Age	Sex	Race	Profession	Birth Place
Crabtree,	Jesse	38	M	W	Farmer	TN
	Julia A.	36	F	W		TN
	Wilber	14	M	W		TN
	Mary	12	F	W		KY
	Isaac	10	M	W		TN
	Riza	7	F	W		TN
	Caleb	2	M	W		TN
Bruster,	James	62	M	W	Blacksmith	VA
	Phebe	60	F	W		VA
	James G.	34	M	W	Farm Laborer	TN
	Miller	20	M	W	Farm Laborer	TN
	George W.	17	M	W	Farm Laborer	TN
	Rebeccah	30	F	W		TN
	Barbara E.	14	F	W		TN
	Adaline	8	F	W		TN
	Susanah	4	F	W		TN
	Miller W.	1	M	W		TN
	Nancy L.	41	F	W	Domestic	TN
	Ruthy A.	14	F	W		TN
	Cindrella A.	10	F	W		TN
	Monroe G.	4	M	W		TN
McKinny,	Jesse	51	M	W	Farmer	VA
	Mary	41	F	W		KY
	Elizabeth	20	F	W		KY
	William	14	M	W		KY
	Henry	12	M	W		KY
	John	11	M	W		KY
	Abram	10	M	W		KY
	Wiseman	10	M	W		KY
Sharp,	Joseph	50	M	W		TN
	Sally A.	21	F	W		KY
	Manerva	19	F	W		TN
	William W.	17	M	W		TN
	Isham R.	15	M	W		TN
	Helen M.	13	F	W		TN
	Milley E.	2	F	W		TN

1860 Fentress Co. TN Census

Name		Age Remarks	Sex	Race	Profession	Birth Place

Civil District No. 5
Recorded 24 July 1860

Name		Age	Sex	Race	Profession	Birth Place
Brown,	Abram	23	M	W	Farmer	TN
	John	18	M	W		TN
	Thomas A.	13	M	W		KY
	John Jr.	11	M	W		KY
	Elizabeth	56	F	W	Domestic	KY
Copley,	James	52	M	W	Tenant	NC
	Jane	13	F	W		TN
Copley,	George	37	M	W	Farmer	NC
	Rutha	35	F	W		NC
	Janis L.	13	M	W		TN
	James	3	M	W		TN
	Mary	75	F	W	Domestic	NC
Beason,	James	54	M	W	Farmer	TN
	Mary	40	F	W		TN
Huddleston,	Margaret	20	F	W	Domestic	TN
Beason,	William	18	M	W	Farmer	TN
Huddleston,	James	3	M	W		TN
Waters,	Elijah	17	M	W	Day Laborer	KY
Miller,	Thomas B.	31	M	W	Tenant	NC
	Louisa	27	F	W		NC
	Eli E.	8	M	W		TN
	Martha A.	6	F	W		TN
	Mary J.	3	F	W		KY
	Emeline	1	F	W		TN
Adkinson,	Peter	36	M	W	Tenant	TN
	Sarah E.	33	F	W		TN
	Joel	12	M	W		KY
	William J.	8	M	W		KY
	James C.	7	M	W		KY
	Nancy E.	5	F	W		KY
	Lewis J.	3	M	W		KY
	Viavina E.	11/12	F	W		KY

1860 Fentress Co. TN Census

Name		Age Remarks	Sex	Race	Profession	Birth Place

Civil District No. 5
Recorded 25 July 1860

Name		Age Remarks	Sex	Race	Profession	Birth Place
Sescton,	Hiram	23	M	W	Tenant	TN
	Emmamine A.	18	F	W		KY
Lockett,	John	23	M	W		TN
	Charlotte	23	F	W		TN
	Nancy	3	F	W		TN
	Bordorne	8/12	M	W		TN
Lockett,	Elizabeth	50	F	W	Tenant	VA
	Ava	15	F	W		TN
	Joshua	12	M	W		TN
Lockett,	James	26	M	W	Farmer	TN
	Elizabeth	27	F	W		KY
	Lucinda	2	F	W		TN
	Nancy	8/12	F	W		TN
Doss,	Enins	37	M	W	Farmer	TN
	Ruth	26	F	W		TN
	Nancy	6	F	W		TN
	Washington	3	M	W		TN
	Lytha	1	F	W		TN
Doss,	Nancy	69	F	W	No Occupation	NC
	Sarah	29	F	W	Day Laborer	TN
	Amanda C.	5	F	W		TN
	Alvira	2	F	W		TN
	Aaron	2/12	M	W		TN

1860 Fentress Co. TN Census

Name		Age Remarks	Sex	Race	Profession	Birth Place

Civil District No. 6
Recorded 2 July 1860

Name		Age	Sex	Race	Profession	Birth Place
Poor,	James	28	M	W	Tenant	TN
	Mary A.	27	F	W		TN
	Jeremiah	10	M	W		TN
	Jane	7	F	W		TN
	Nancy	5	F	W		TN
	Henry	2	M	W		TN
	William	6/12	M	W		TN
Singleton,	?	72	F	W	Farming	VA
Brock,	A. B.	36	M	W	Tenant	TN
	Mary A.	28	F	W		TN
	Martha	3	F	W		TN
	Abner	1/12	M	W		TN
Singleton,	Elizabeth	17	F	W	Domestic	TN
	Kiza	11	F	W		TN
Bond,	Samuel	55	M	W	Farmer	KY
	Nancy	51	F	W		VA
	Francis J.	24	F	W		KY
	James G.	22	M	W		KY
	Marionatte	21	F	W		KY
	Eliza A.	21	F	W		KY
	Emily S.	19	F	W		KY
	Elias T.	18	M	W		KY
	Perry G.	13	M	W		KY
	Kimble M.	13	M	W		KY
	John S. J. R.	9	M	W		KY
	Melinda	3	F	W		KY
Buch,	Catharine J.	26	F	W	Domestic	KY
	Sarah	9/12	F	W		TN
Hisan,	Henry	21	M	W	Day Laborer	TN
Young,	James	38	M	W	Farmer	TN
	Jane	30	F	W		TN
	Ewn	14	M	W		TN
	James Mc	11	M	W		TN
	Anna	9	F	W		TN
	Jeremiah	7	M	W		TN
	Pradine	4	F	W		TN
	Nancy C.	2	F	W		TN

1860 Fentress Co. TN Census

Name		Age Remarks	Sex	Race	Profession	Birth Place

Civil District No. 6
Recorded 2 July 1860

Name		Age Remarks	Sex	Race	Profession	Birth Place
Noland,	Elijah	63	M	W	Farmer	TN
	Mary	63	F	W		VA
Campbell,	D. C.	23	M	W	Tenant	TN
	Elizabeth C.	21	F	W		KY
	John C.	3	M	W		MO
Hill,	Wm. R.	26	M	W	Tenant	TN
	Elizabeth	18	F	W		TN
	John P.	2	M	W		TN
	Unnamed	1	M	W		TN
	Nancy	50	F	W	Domestic	NC
	Pervina P.	20	F	W	Domestic	TN
	George L.	15	M	W	Day Laborer	TN
Hison,	Frederick	57	M	W	Farmer	NC
Padgett,	Elizabeth	53	F	W	Domestic	NC
Payne,	James M.	38	M	W	Farmer	TN
	Elizabeth	38	F	W		TN
	Mary	8	F	W		TN
	Mary	46	F	W	Domestic	TN
Smith,	Isaac D.	50	M	W	Farmer	KY
	Zenelda A.	46	F	W		KY
	Elizabeth J.	25	F	W		AL
	Milly A.	20	F	W		TN
	John M.	18	M	W	Farmer	TN
	Jonathan L.	15	M	W		TN
	Mary V.	13	F	W		TN
	Martha M.	11	F	W		TN
	Nancy A.	9	F	W		TN
	Isaac Woolsey	7	M	W		TN
	William L.	5	M	W		TN
	Philip	90	M	W	Farmer	VA
	Milly	81	F	W		VA

1860 Fentress Co. TN Census

Name		Age Remarks	Sex	Race	Profession	Birth Place

Civil District No. 6
Recorded 2 July 1860

Name		Age Remarks	Sex	Race	Profession	Birth Place
Harris,	George A.	34	M	W	Farmer	TN
	Louisa	32	F	W		TN
	Joseph D.	13	M	W		TN
	Mary	11	F	W		TN
	Martha?	6	F	W		TN
	Amanda	3	F	W		TN
Hildreth,	Abner	27	M	W	Farmer	TN
	Mary A.	21	F	W		TN
	Van	3/12	M	W		TN
	Alsa	46	F	W	Domestic	KY
	William	17	M	W	Farm Hand	TN
	Joseph	14	M	W		TN
Felkins,	Joel M.	50	M	W	Farmer	KY
	Dililah	48	F	W		TN
	James A.	21	M	W	Farmer	TN
	William H.	19	M	W	Farmer	TN
	Eliza J. C.	17	F	W		TN
	Joel M.	15	M	W		TN
	Feriba H.	7	F	W		TN
	John M.	4	M	W		TN
Gunning,	Joseph M.	22	M	W	Tenant	TN
	Elizabeth A.	23	F	W		TN
Wills,	Anderson	34	M	W	Farmer	KY
	Lydia	32	F	W		KY
	Leslie C.	11	M	W		KY
	Clarinda F.	7	F	W		TN
	Irene E.	6	F	W		TN
	Mary A.	3	F	W		TN
	Virginia O.	1	F	W		KY
Singleton,	Peter	47	M	W	Farmer	VA
	Louisa	34	F	W		VA
	James S.	19	M	W	Farmer	VA
	Melissa	14	F	W		VA
	Martha	12	F	W		VA
	John T.	8	M	W		VA
	Elizabeth E.	6	F	W		VA
	Lavina V.	2	F	W		TN

1860 Fentress Co. TN Census

Name		Age Remarks	Sex	Race	Profession	Birth Place

Civil District No. 6
Recorded 2 July 1860

Name		Age Remarks	Sex	Race	Profession	Birth Place
Hair,	James	63	M	W	Farmer	KY
	Elizabeth	56	F	W		KY
Lastre,	Emeline	33	F	W	Domestic	KY
Hair,	Comfort	18	F	W		KY
	Milly	16	F	W		KY
	Henry	13	M	W		KY
	Nancy	10	F	W		KY
Lastre,	Elizabeth	7	F	W		KY
	William	5	M	W		KY
	James	3	M	W		KY
Wright,	David	46	M	W	Farmer	VA
	Mary	46	F	W		TN
	Melinda	19	F	W		TN
	Margaret	17	F	W		TN
Zackery,	James A.	46	M	W	Farmer	TN
	Cassandee	46	F	W		TN
	Mary A.	24	F	W		TN
	Peter A.	21	M	W	Farmer	TN
	James M.	19	M	W	Farmer	TN
	Mitchel P.	18	M	W	Farmer	TN
	Esther	16	F	W	Farmer	TN
	William L.	14	M	W		TN
	Saml T.	12	M	W		TN
	Pearson M.	10	M	W		TN
	Permila	8	F	W		TN
	Lafayette	6	M	W		TN
	Dillard	3	M	W		TN
Huddleston,	Ambrose F.	28	M	W	Tenant	TN
	Lucinda	28	F	W		TN
	Moses	4	M	W		TN
	Martha	3	F	W		TN
	Joseph	4/12	M	W		TN

1860 Fentress Co. TN Census

Name		Age Remarks	Sex	Race	Profession	Birth Place

Civil District No. 6
Recorded 2 July 1860

Name		Age	Sex	Race	Profession	Birth Place
Hunt,	Moses	33	M	W	Farmer	KY
	Julia A.	28	F	W		KY
	Mary	8	F	W		KY
	Sina J.	7	F	W		KY
	Henry C.	5	M	W		KY
	Thomas C.	4	M	W		KY
	William A.	1	M	W		TN
Storie,	Joshua	33	M	W	Farmer	TN
	Celia J.	37	F	W		TN
	Jonathan W.	5	M	W		TN
	Mary J.	3	F	W		TN
	Thomas J.	9/12	M	W		TN
Harris,	Sarah M.	15	F	W	Domestic	TN
	James H.	13	M	W		TN
Jeffres,	Thomas L.	29	M	W	Tenant	TN
Hicks,	Thomas M.	23	M	W	Farmer	KY
	Louisa	22	F	W		KY
	Julia A.	3	F	W		KY
	Clarinda J.	1	F	W		KY
Harris,	Joseph	79	M	W	Miller	TN
Allen,	A. M.	55	M	W	Farmer	NC
	Elina	52	F	W		NC
	A. L.	17	M	W	Teacher	NC
Stewart,	Anna	32	F	W	Domestic	TN
	Joseph	8	M	W		TN
Singleton,	William	44	M	W	Farmer	VA
	Milly	40	F	W		TN
Frogge,	Permelia	14	F	W		KY
Singleton,	Sarah	13	F	W		TN
Frogge,	Jonathan	9	M	W		KY
Smith,	Samuel	59	M	W	Farmer	VA
	Amanda	44	F	W		KY
	Mary E.	3	F	W		TN

1860 Fentress Co. TN Census

Name		Age Remarks	Sex	Race	Profession	Birth Place

Civil District No. 6
Recorded 2 July 1860

Name		Age	Sex	Race	Profession	Birth Place
Dickson,	James A.	25	M	W	Tenant	KY
	Catharine	27	F	W		TN
	Adela A.	5	F	W		TN
	William A.	1	M	W		TN
Bayter,	Elizabeth	77	F	W	Gardening	TN
Poor,	J. O.	40	M	W	Farmer	TN
Moredock,	Sarah M.	37	F	W	Domestic	TN
	George	8	M	W		TN
Poor,	Henry R.	50	M	W	Farmer	TN
	Lucy	45	F	W		KY
	Samuel	14	M	W		TN
	Frederick	12	M	W		TN
	Jeremiah	10	M	W		TN
	Mary	8	F	W		TN
	Henry	3	M	W		TN

Recorded 3 July 1860

Name		Age	Sex	Race	Profession	Birth Place
Cannon,	Henry M.	29	M	W	Miller	TN
	Priseilla	27	F	W		KY
	Maria C.	10	F	W		KY
	Mary	8	F	W		KY
	Susan	8	F	W		KY
	Jane	6	F	W		KY
	Luvina	5	F	W		KY
	Emalia	3	F	W		KY
	G. W.	1	M	W		KY
Gains,	James	26	M	W	Tenant	TN
	Susan	20	F	W		TN
	William	7	M	W		TN
	Sarah E.	5	F	W		TN
	Mary S.	3	F	W		TN
	James C.	1	M	W		TN
Buck,	Peter	26	M	W	Tenant	TN

1860 Fentress Co. TN Census

Name		Age Remarks	Sex	Race	Profession	Birth Place

Civil District No. 6
Recorded 3 July 1860

Name		Age	Sex	Race	Profession	Birth Place
Young,	Mathew	32	M	W	Farmer	TN
	Anna	64	F	W	Domestic	TN
	Nancy	23	F	W	Domestic	TN
	Randy C.	21	F	W	Domestic	TN
	Martin	21	M	W	Farmer	TN
Jackson,	J. C.	52	M	W	Tenant	TN
	Luvina	48	F	W		TN
	Margaret L.	18	F	W		TN
	Sarah M.	17	F	W	Tenant	TN
	Moses H.	15	M	W		TN
	James S.	13	M	W		TN
	C. R.	12	M	W		TN
	Feriba A.	10	F	W		TN
	John G.	9	M	W		TN
	Robert L.	7	M	W		TN
	Lucinda L.	5	M	W		TN
Buck,	Benjamin	58	M	W	Farmer	NC
	Sarah	57	F	W		TN
	John	32	M	W	Wagon Worker	TN
	Mary	24	F	W		TN
	Hily	21	F	W		TN
	Miles	19	M	W	Farmer	TN
Wright,	A. B.	33	M	W		TN
	Cinthia	32	F	W		TN
	Mary J.	9	F	W		TN
	James C.	8	M	W		TN
Flowers,	Manson	35	M	W	?	TN
	Lucinda	45	F	W		TN
	Martha J.	26	F	W		TN
	Margaret M.	24	F	W		TN
	Nancy	12	F	W		TN
	Pearson	11	M	W		TN
	Susan M.	8	F	W		TN
	Elizabeth	7	F	W		TN
	John F.	7	M	W		KY
Evens,	Susan	63	F	W	Domestic	VA

1860 Fentress Co. TN Census

Name		Age Remarks	Sex	Race	Profession	Birth Place

Civil District No. 6
Recorded 3 July 1860

Name		Age	Sex	Race	Profession	Birth Place
Harmon,	Ruben	27	M	W	Farmer	TN
	Emeline	25	F	W		TN
	John	5	M	W		TN
	George	3	M	W		TN
	Rebeccah	1	F	W		TN
Page,	John S.	43	M	W	Doctor	VA
	Elanisa	36	F	W		KY
	Titus	18	M	W	Farmer	KY
	Ann L.	15	F	W		KY
	Lucy E.	13	F	W		KY
	Mary M.	10	F	W		KY
	Sam J.	9	M	W		KY
	Robert L.	6	M	W		TN
	Emma D.	2	F	W		TN
Rice,	E. B.	24	M	W	Medical Student	KY
Thompson,	Henry	45	M	W	Farmer	VA
	Lily	55	F	W		VA
	Alfred	12	M	W		TN
Frogge,	James M.	28	M	W	Tenant	TN
	Eliza J.	28	F	W		TN
	Samuel	8	M	W		TN
	James T.	6	F	W		TN
	Evan D.	4	M	W		TN
	John B.	1	M	W		KY

Recorded 4 July 1860

Name		Age	Sex	Race	Profession	Birth Place
Evens,	S. D.	30	M	W	Farmer	TN
	Louisa	26	F	W		TN
	Mary	7	F	W		TN
	Amanda	6	F	W		TN
	Canzada	4	F	W		TN
	Sarah	3	F	W		TN
	Taylor B.	9/12	M	W		TN

1860 Fentress Co. TN Census

Name		Age Remarks	Sex	Race	Profession	Birth Place	

Civil District No. 6
Recorded 4 July 1860

Name		Age Remarks	Sex	Race	Profession	Birth Place	
Crouch,	E. H.	28	M	W	Farmer	KY	
	Susan	27	F	W		KY	
	Alendsine	8	M	W		TN	
	John W.	5	M	W		TN	
	Anginome	3	F	W		TN	
	James A.	1	M	W		TN	
Witt,	Samuel	40	M	W	Tenant	TN	
	Jane	36	F	W		TN	
	Maria E.	15	F	W		TN	
	James D.	13	M	W		TN	
	Milissa A.	8	F	W		TN	
	Charles L.	6	M	W		TN	
	Wesley R.	3	M	W		TN	
	Vestina A.	6/12	F	W		TN	
McDonnald,	William B.	49	M	W	Farmer	TN	
	Martha E.	40	F	W		KY	
	J. L.	18	M	W	Farmer	TN	
	B. C. T.	16	M	W	Farmer	TN	
	Isaac L.	15	M	W	Farmer	TN	
	Samuel W.	12	M	W		TN	
	Philip E.	11	M	W		TN	
	William L.	8	M	W		TN	
	John S.	6	M	W		TN	
	Frances J.	5	F	W		TN	
	Mary S.	10/12	F	W		TN	
Caltian,	Martha E.	16	F	W	Domestic	TN	
McDonnald,	Elizabeth	87	F	W	Domestic	TN	Blind
Smith,	John C.	28	M	W	Tenant	KY	
	Martha	28	F	W		KY	
	Levina M.	7	F	W		TN	
	Samuel B.	4	M	W		TN	
	Vestina	3	F	W		TN	
Litterd,	Samuel	30	M	W	Farmer	KY	
	Elizabeth	30	F	W		KY	
	Mary J.	8	F	W		KY	
	George R.	6	M	W		KY	
	Thomas L.	5	M	W		KY	

1860 Fentress Co. TN Census

Name		Age Remarks	Sex	Race	Profession	Birth Place	

Civil District No. 6
Recorded 4 July 1860

Name		Age	Sex	Race	Profession	Birth Place	
Jeff,	William	31	M	W		KY	Insane
	Eddy	48	F	W		KY	
Davidson,	William C.	39	M	W	Stone Mason	TN	
	Nancy	37	F	W		TN	
	Willis T.	17	M	W	Farmer	TN	
	Mary L.	16	F	W		TN	
	Milton W.	14	M	W		TN	
	Kiza I.	10	F	W		TN	
	Sibina? E.	8	F	W		TN	
	J. B.	5	M	W		TN	
	Pernetta	3	F	W		TN	
	Margaret C.	1	F	W		TN	
Conatser,	L. D.	44	M	W	Farmer	NC	
	Mary	57	F	W		VA	
	Elizabeth	24	F	W		KY	
	Lavina?	21	F	W		KY	
	Jacob	17	M	W	Farmer	KY	
	Joseph	14	M	W		KY	
	Leanna	75	F	W	Domestic	NC	
Dishman,	Moses	43	M	W	Farmer	NC	
	Milly	43	F	W		NC	
	Serena C.	20	F	W		KY	
	Raina G.	18	F	W		KY	
	Mary J.	14	F	W		KY	
	Louisa	12	F	W		KY	
	Ruben S.	10	M	W		KY	
	Clenianza W.	4	F	W		KY	
	Lucinda N.	2	F	W		KY	
Evens,	Alexander	34	M	W	Farmer	TN	
	Sara	35	F	W		KY	
	Pearson	12	M	W		TN	
	Thetney	10	F	W		TN	
	Melissa	8	F	W		TN	
	Robert	6	M	W		TN	
	Stephen	4	M	W		TN	
	Mary J.	2	F	W		TN	

1860 Fentress Co. TN Census

Name		Age Remarks	Sex	Race	Profession	Birth Place

Civil District No. 6
Recorded 4 July 1860

Name		Age Remarks	Sex	Race	Profession	Birth Place
Evens,	Floyd	34	M	W	Tenant	TN
	Margaret	33	F	W		KY
	Calvin	12	M	W		TN
	Alfred	10	M	W		TN
	Amanda	8	F	W		TN
	Nancy	6	F	W		TN
	William	4	M	W		TN
	Sarah A.	7/12	F	W		TN
Campbell,	John	53	M	W	Farmer	VA
	Margaret	49	F	W		KY
	Sarah A. S.	20	F	W		TN
	James	17	M	W	Farmer	TN
	I. D.	15	M	W	Farmer	TN
	Jesse	11	M	W		TN
	Martha V. I.	9	F	W		TN
	Adela	6	F	W		TN

Recorded 5 July 1860

Name		Age Remarks	Sex	Race	Profession	Birth Place
Wilson,	Jonathan	37	M	W	Miller	TN
	Catharine	39	F	W		VA
	Mary J.	17	F	W		KY
	Margaret E.	15	F	W		KY
	Samuel S.	12	M	W		KY
	Benjamin M. D.	9	M	W		KY
	Matilda C.	9	F	W		KY
	Adam H.	8	M	W		TN
	Nancy V.	6	F	W		TN
	Timothy T. B.	4	M	W		TN
	Jonathan J.	2	M	W		TN
Clarborne,	James B.	53	M	W	Tenant	VA
	Emeline C.	30	F	W		TN
	Amanda	9	F	W		TN
	William	7	M	W		TN
	James	5	M	W		TN
	John	3	M	W		TN
	Edward	1	M	W		TN
Flowers,	Lurania	10	F	W		TN

1860 Fentress Co. TN Census

Name		Age Remarks	Sex	Race	Profession	Birth Place
Scorling,	Richard	26	M	W	Tenant	TN
	Eliza J.	27	F	W		TN
	George W.	7	M	W		TN
	Lucy C.	6	F	W		TN
	Flora A.	3	F	W		KY
	John M.	2	M	W		KY
	Hester J.	4/12	F	W		TN
Smith,	Lucy A.	14	F	W	Domestic	TN
Smith,	George P.	55	M	W	Tenant	KY
	Lucy	55	F	W		TN
	Samantha M.	21	F	W		TN
	James L.	7/12	M	W		TN
Hildreth,	P. M.	37	M	W	Farmer	IN
	Lucinda	35	F	W		TN
	Caroline	16	F	W		TN
	Thornson H.	14	M	W		TN
	Alcy	12	F	W		TN
	Jeffrey	10	M	W		TN
	Reese	8	M	W		TN
	Malinda E.	5	F	W		TN
	Amanda	3	F	W		TN
Cornelius,	Nicholas	59	M	W	Farmer	KY
	Rachel	49	F	W		TN
Brock,	G. A.	33	M	W	Farm Tenant	TN
	Louisa J.	23	F	W		TN
	Francis M.	13	M	W		TN
	George A.	12	M	W		TN
	Rachel A.	11	F	W		TN
	Mary A.	9	F	W		TN
	Martha R.	7	F	W		TN
	William M.	4	M	W		TN
	James D.	1	M	W		TN

Civil District No. 6
Recorded 5 July 1860

1860 Fentress Co. TN Census

Name		Age Remarks	Sex	Race	Profession	Birth Place

Civil District No. 6
Recorded 5 July 1860

Name		Age	Sex	Race	Profession	Birth Place
Sylvia,	Nicholas	54	M	W	Wagon Maker	PA
	Mary C.	34	F	W		PA
	Mary M.	17	F	W		PA
	Samuel M.	6	M	W		KY
	Pansy D.	4	M	W		TN
	Hannah M.	2	F	W		KY
Rector,	James	35	M	W	Farmer	KY
	Mary	32	F	W		KY
	Samuel W.	7	M	W		KY
	Albert L.	7/12	M	W		TN
Sanders,	George H.	16	M	W	Domestic	KY
Hale,	Jonathan	43	M	W	Doctor	NH
	Feriba A.	36	F	W		TN
	Jonathan D.	16	M	W	Farmer	TN
	Sarah H.	14	F	W		TN
	Feriba A.	12	F	W		TN
	Gertrude	8	F	W		TN
	Susan	3	F	W		TN
	Henry H.	10/12	M	W		TN
Flowers,	William	73	M	W	Farmer	VA
	Clarissa	35	F	W		TN
	Franky	7	F	W		TN
	Juda	6	F	W		TN
	Mary M.	4	F	W		TN
	William	3	M	W		TN
	Mary	1	F	W		TN
Kerney,	Lucinda	42	F	W	Weaver	TN
	Mary	19	F	W		TN
	William	15	M	W	Day Laborer	TN
	Lavina	12	F	W		TN
	Eliza	10	F	W		TN
	Matilda	7	F	W		TN
	Samuel	5	M	W		TN
	Elizabeth	3	F	W		TN

1860 Fentress Co. TN Census

Name		Age Remarks	Sex	Race	Profession	Birth Place

Civil District No. 6
Recorded 6 July 1860

Name		Age	Sex	Race	Profession	Birth Place
Dowdy,	Rufus	41	M	W	Carpenter	NC
	Catharine	36	F	W		TN
	Mary A.	21	F	W		MO
	Louisa J.	19	F	W		MO
	Pernetta	16	F	W		MO
	Perry O.	15	M	W	Farmer	TN
	Catharine C.	13	F	W		TN
	Jackson	11	M	W		TN
	Magga M.	9	F	W		TN
	Ellen M.	7	F	W		TN
	Jacob A.	4	M	W		TN
	Susan V.	1	F	W		TN
Walker,	William	41	M	W	Mechanic	TN
	Matilda	20	F	W		KY
	James S.	5	M	W		TN
	John B.	3	M	W		TN
	Robert W.	6/12	M	W		TN
Walker,	Nathaniel	27	M	W	Farmer	TN
	Nancy	38	F	W	Domestic	TN
	Elizabeth	36	F	W	Domestic	TN
	Mahala V.	26	F	W	Domestic	TN
Walker,	Robert	50	M	W	Tenant	VA
	Sarah	45	F	W		TN
	Archabald B.	21	M	W	Tenant	TN
	Nancy J.	20	F	W		TN
	Elizabeth	18	F	W		TN
	Delia	16	F	W		TN
	Mary	14	F	W		TN
	Louisa H.	12	F	W		TN
	Joyseia H.	9	F	W		TN
	Sarah E.	7	F	W		TN
	James M.	5	M	W		TN
	Margaret S.	2	F	W		TN

1860 Fentress Co. TN Census

Name		Age Remarks	Sex	Race	Profession	Birth Place
		Civil District No. 6				
		Recorded 6 July 1860				
Hisan,	Frederic	25	M	W	Tenant	TN
	Anna	26	F	W		TN
	Mahala J.	7	F	W		TN
	Henry	5	M	W		KY
	Catharine	3	F	W		TN
	General S.	6/12	M	W		TN
Zackery,	John	56	M	W	Farmer	TN
	Nancy	53	F	W		TN
	Caroline	23	F	W		TN
	Pleasant	18	M	W	Farmer	TN
	John N.	16	M	W	Farmer	TN
	Milton M.	13	M	W		TN
	Jane	10	F	W		TN
Clarborne,	Robert	41	M	W	Farmer	TN
	Hannah	31	F	W		TN
	Leonard	13	M	W		TN
	John	10	M	W		TN
	Stephen	8	M	W		TN
	Francis	6	F	W		TN
	Nancy	3	F	W		TN
	Mary	2	F	W		TN
Dickson,	Jane	55	F	W	Gardening	TN
	Martha	27	F	W		TN
	Elsey C.	16	F	W		TN
Claeborne,	Stephen	36	M	W	Turner	TN
	Josephine	24	F	W		TN
	Mary A.	8	F	W		TN
	Cornelius N.	6	M	W		TN
	Robert T.	4	M	W		TN
	Rachel A. D.	2	F	W		TN
	Martha C.	6/12	F	W		TN

1860 Fentress Co. TN Census

Name		Age Remarks	Sex	Race	Profession	Birth Place

Civil District No. 6
Recorded 6 July 1860

Name		Age	Sex	Race	Profession	Birth Place
Norris,	William P.	35	M	W	Farmer	NC
	Anna	39	F	W		TN
	Malvina A.	8	F	W		TN
	James F.	7	M	W		TN
	Armemas	5	M	W		TN
	John H.	2	M	W		TN
	Louisa B. T.	11/12	F	W		TN
Nichalas,	Sarah	38	F	W	Farming	TN
	Jeremiah A.	8	M	W		TN
	Cornilius C.	7	M	W		TN
	George H.	5	M	W		TN
Huddleston,	Mary	21	F	W	Domestic	TN
Simpson,	Brackston D.	53	M	W	Farmer	OH
	Milly	45	F	W		TN
	Roanna	17	F	W		TN
	Edward E.	16	M	W	Farmer	TN
	Martha	13	F	W		TN
	William B.	11	M	W		TN
	Winnie J.	9	F	W		TN
	Sarah E.	5	F	W		TN
	Mary A.	3	F	W		TN
Huddleston,	C. A.	28	M	W	Farmer	TN
	Malvina J.	20	F	W		TN
	C. W.	3	M	W		TN
	Sarah L.	1	F	W		TN

1860 Fentress Co. TN Census

Name		Age Remarks	Sex	Race	Profession	Birth Place

Civil District No. 7
Recorded 9 July 1860

Name		Age	Sex	Race	Profession	Birth Place
Putt,	John F.	4?	M	W	Farmer	TN
	Livinah	44	F	W		TN
	Eli	26	M	W	Miller	TN
	George W.	20	M	W	Farmer	TN
	Joel	18	M	W	Farmer	TN
	Jackson	16	M	W	Farmer	TN
Mullinix,	Sampson	14	M	W		TN
	Samuel W.	10	M	W		TN
	William	8	M	W		TN
	Nina E.	6	F	W		TN
Frogge,	John S.	31	M	W	Tenant	TN
	Susanah	35	F	W		TN
	E. D.	11	M	W		TN
	Esther A.	10	F	W		TN
	John F.	8	M	W		TN
	Prudence J.	5	F	W		TN
	Tennessee	2	F	W		TN
	George W.	6/12	M	W		TN
Moles,	Henry	24	M	W	Tenant	TN
	Elizabeth	23	F	W		TN
	Catharine	?	F	W		TN
	Mary A.	1	F	W		TN
Moles,	David	57	M	W	Farmer	VA
	Sarah	47	F	W		TN
	Elizabeth	19	F	W		TN
	George W.	17	M	W	Farmer	TN
	Elijah	15	M	W	Farmer	TN
	Matilda	13	F	W		TN
	Sarah	11	F	W		TN
	Nelson	9	M	W		TN
	Celia	8	F	W		TN
	Anna	6	F	W		TN
	Malvina	3	F	W		TN
	Catharine	16	F	W		TN
Davidson,	Thomas	6	M	W		TN

1860 Fentress Co. TN Census

Name		Age Remarks	Sex	Race	Profession	Birth Place
		Civil District No. 7				
		Recorded 9 July 1860				
Bookout,	James	59	M	W	Farmer	TN
	Sarah	53	F	W		NC
	Rachel	32	F	W		TN
	Eliza	30	F	W		TN
	William	28	M	W	Farmer	TN
	John C.	25	M	W	Farmer	TN
	James M.	22	M	W	Farmer	TN
	Sarah	20	F	W		TN
	Dililah E.	16	F	W		TN
	Isaac W.	13	M	W		TN
	Mary J.	11	F	W		TN
Duncan,	John	49	M	W	Farmer	TN
	Lucretia	37	F	W		TN
	Philip	22	M	W	Farmer	TN
	Janis B.	20	M	W	Farmer	TN
	James J.	19	M	W	Farmer	TN
	Hiram M.	14	M	W		TN
	Allen	12	M	W		TN
	Margaret	9	F	W		TN
	John F. P.	7	M	W		TN
	Mary E.	4	F	W		TN
	Caleb	1	M	W		TN
Cverelious?,	W. E.	39	M	W	Farmer	TN
	Susanah	35	F	W		TN
	J. C.	14	M	W		TN
	N. W.	11	M	W		TN
	Sarah J.	9	F	W		TN
	Nancy A. E.	6	F	W		TN
	G. P.	4	M	W		TN
	A. C.	2	F	W		TN

1860 Fentress Co. TN Census

Name		Age Remarks	Sex	Race	Profession	Birth Place
		Civil District No. 7				
		Recorded 9 July 1860				
Poor,	James	50	M	W	Farmer	TN
	Dililah	49	F	W		KY
	Jane F.	22	F	W		TN
	John T.	20	M	W	Farmer	TN
	Person M.	17	M	W	Farmer	TN
	Pleasant	14	M	W		TN
	Jeremiah	11	M	W		TN
	James	8	M	W		TN
	Armsted M.	6	M	W		TN
	Dililah J.	4	F	W		TN
Simm,	Manda A. M.	17	F	W	Domestic	TN
Fite,	Peter	57	M	W	Farmer	NC
	Elizabeth	50	F	W		TN
	Cinthia A.	18	F	W		TN
	Mary L.	17	F	W		TN
	John	14	M	W		TN
	Nancy J.	12	F	W		TN
	Jerminia L. M.	10	F	W		TN
	Frances E.	8	F	W		TN
Green,	Newton	27	M	W	Tenant	TN
	Sarah M.	27	F	W		TN
	Saloma L. A.	1	F	W		TN
Buck,	Martha	32	F	W	Tenant	TN
	Mary	15	F	W		TN
	James	14	M	W		TN
	Margaret	11	F	W		TN
	Catharine	9	F	W		TN
	Thomas	7	M	W		TN
	Stokely	5	M	W		TN
	Eliza J.	2	F	W		TN
Griffin,	Joseph	39	M	W	Tenant	KY
	Margaret	36	F	W		TN
	Eliza A.	13	F	W		TN
	William	12	M	W		TN
	John	10	M	W		TN
	Joseph	7	M	W		TN

1860 Fentress Co. TN Census

Name		Age Remarks	Sex	Race	Profession	Birth Place

Civil District No. 7
Recorded 9 July 1860

Name		Age	Sex	Race	Profession	Birth Place
Evans,	Joshua S.	38	M	W	Farmer	TN
	Genetta	30	F	W		TN
	Elizabeth	8	F	W		TN
	Margaret	4	F	W		TN
	Mary	6/12	F	W		TN
Birton,	Benjamin	24	M	W	Tenant	TN
	Margaret	23	F	W		TN
	Martha	5/12	F	W		TN
Locher,	Granvill	25	M	W	Tenant	KY
	Thomas	22	M	W	Tenant	KY
	Elmira	21	F	W		KY
	Catharine	19	F	W		KY
	William	16	M	W	Tenant	KY
	Catharine	11	F	W		KY
	Martha J.	10	F	W		KY
	Joanna	2	F	W		KY
	Pernetta	20	F	W	Domestic	KY
	Nelly	57	F	W	Domestic	NC
Wallis,	Thomas	16	M	W	Day Laborer	KY
Wilson,	Jacob	49	M	W	Tenant	TN
	Dorathy	49	F	W		VA
	Mary A.	15	F	W		TN
	Rebeccah	14	F	W		TN
	Lucinda	10	F	W		TN
	Jackson	23	M	W	Farming	TN

Recorded 10 July 1860

Name		Age	Sex	Race	Profession	Birth Place
Crouch,	Rhoda A.	30	F	W	Farmer	TN
	Luvina	13	F	W		TN
	Machariah T.	12	M	W		TN
	Vestina	10	F	W		TN
	Dudly	8	M	W		TN
	Joseph	7	M	W		TN
	Elizabeth J.	5	F	W		TN

1860 Fentress Co. TN Census

Name		Age Remarks	Sex	Race	Profession	Birth Place

Civil District No. 7
Recorded 10 July 1860

Name		Age	Sex	Race	Profession	Birth Place
Buck,	Thomas Sr.	81	M	W	Farmer	PA
	Mary	72	F	W		TN
	Noah	33	M	W	Shoe Maker	TN
	Anna	30	F	W		TN
	Didoma	10	F	W		TN
	Mary	8	F	W		TN
	Elizabeth	6	F	W		TN
	Rutha	4	F	W		FN
Evans,	Matilda	40	F	W	Tenant	TN
	Amanda	17	F	W		TN
	Mary M.	15	F	W		TN
	Ewing S.	13	M	W		TN
	Elizabeth	10	F	W		TN
	Joseph S.	8	M	W		TN
	Margaret S.	6	F	W		TN
Pevyhouse,	George	49	M	W	Farmer	TN
	Rachel	30	F	W		TN
	John	22	M	W	Farmer	TN
	Abram	17	M	W	Farmer	TN
	George W.	16	M	W	Farmer	TN
	Margaret	12	F	W		TN
	Caroline	10	F	W		TN
	Marion	8	M	W		TN
Riley,	John F.	45	M	W	Farmer	TN
	Elizabeth	30	F	W		TN
	John B.	19	M	W		TN
	Rebeccah	16	F	W		TN
	Nancy	12	F	W		TN
	Caleb	9	M	W		TN
	Luan	3	F	W		TN
Brown,	Selina	23	F	W	Domestic	NC
Wilson,	Jackson	30	M	W	Tenant	TN
	Martha	29	F	W		TN
	Sarah	6	F	W		TN
	Jacob L.	1	M	W		TN
	Nancy	70	F	W	Domestic	TN

1860 Fentress Co. TN Census

Name		Age Remarks	Sex	Race	Profession	Birth Place

Name		Age	Sex	Race	Profession	Birth Place
Angilly,	Alfred	41	M	W		TN
	Martha	36	F	W		TN
	Sarah J.	14	F	W		TN
	Thomas	12	M	W		TN
	Mary	10	F	W		TN
	Isaac M.	8	M	W		TN
	Elizabeth N.	6	F	W		TN
	John F.	3	M	W		TN
	Alexander	5/12	M	W		TN
Johnson,	Asa	52	M	W	Farmer	NC
	Rebeccah J.	39	F	W		TN
	Francis M.	24	M	W	Farmer	TN
	Julius	22	M	W	Farmer	TN
	John A.	10	M	W		TN
	Julian	8	F	W		TN
	Gilford D.	6	M	W		TN
	Melvin M. L.	3	M	W		TN
Hughs,	Sarah A. E.	22	F	W	Domestic	TN
Rich,	William	47	M	W	Farmer	TN
	Mary	44	F	W		TN
	Amanda	15	F	W		TN
	Thomas J.	13	M	W		TN
	Jonathan	11	M	W		TN
	Matilda	10	F	W		TN
	Margaret	8	F	W		TN
	Mary E.	11/12	F	W		TN
Rich,	Catharine	72	F	W	No Occupation	NC
Rich,	James	41	M	W	Farmer	TN
	Mary A.	28	F	W		TN
	John P.	5	M	W		TN
	Francis M.	4	M	W		TN
	Albert	1	M	W		TN

1860 Fentress Co. TN Census

Name		Age Remarks	Sex	Race	Profession	Birth Place

Civil District No. 7
Recorded 10 July 1860

Name		Age	Sex	Race	Profession	Birth Place
Reed,	Emeline	29	F	W	Farmer	KY
	Martha	8	F	W		TN
	Thersa	7	F	W		TN
	Adam	3	M	W		TN
	James	1	M	W		TN
Millsaps,	Elizabeth	60	F	W	Domestic	NC
Reed,	Joseph C.	25	M	W	Farmer	TN
	Sarah E.	24	F	W		KY
	Jame N.	3	M	W		TN
	Martha L.	1	F	W		TN
Choate,	Sabe	36	M	W	Farmer	TN
	Sarah	35	F	W		TN
	Edward	9	M	W		TN
	William	8	M	W		TN
	Isaac	4	M	W		TN
	George	11	M	W		TN

Recorded 11 July 1860

Name		Age	Sex	Race	Profession	Birth Place
Rohm,	Isaac	73	M	W	Miller	VA
	Elizabeth	48	F	W		NC
	Nancy	18	F	W		TN
	Tennessee	16	F	W		TN
	Julia Ann	13	F	W		TN
	William O.	9	M	W		TN
Kidd,	William	33	M	W	Farmer	TN
	Jane	35	M	W		TN
	Mary E.	11	F	W		TN
	Alsa L.	9	F	W		TN
	Milly A.	7	F	W		TN
	Margaret J.	5	F	W		TN
	Clemnontine	2	F	W		TN
Gilreath,	William A.	31	M	W	Farmer	NC
	Mary A.	30	F	W		NC
	Martha E.	11	F	W		TN
	Elina A.	7	F	W		TN
	Melissa A.	4	F	W		TN

1860 Fentress Co. TN Census

Name		Age Remarks	Sex	Race	Profession	Birth Place

Civil District No. 7
Recorded 11 July 1860

Name		Age Remarks	Sex	Race	Profession	Birth Place
Moody,	Green C.	27	M	W	Farmer	TN
	Louisa L. J.	30	F	W		TN
	John	8	M	W		TN
	Margaret A. P.	6	F	W		TN
	Lucinda E.	4	F	W		TN
	Amanda J.	4/12	F	W		TN
Moody,	Benjamin C. T.	26	M	W	Farmer	TN
	Elizabeth A.	21	F	W		TN
	John R.	3	M	W		TN
	James A. R.	1	M	W		TN
	Melissa	13	F	W		TN
Evans,	Jane	42	F	W	Weaver	TN
	Jackson	11	M	W		TN
Davidson,	Wayne	37	M	W	Blacksmith	TN
	Elizabeth	52	F	W	Domestic	TN
	Jonathan S.	23	M	W	Day Laborer	TN
Harmon,	Levi	34	M	W	Farmer	TN
	Thetney	28	F	W		TN
	John F.	11	M	W		TN
	Sarah A.	7	F	W		TN
	Fatima J.	3	F	W		TN
	Margaret	6 days	F	W		TN
Upchurch,	William H.	30	M	W	Farmer	TN
	Caroline	28	F	W		TN
	Mary J.	10	F	W		TN
	Lucinda	7	F	W		TN
	Tiny	3	F	W		KY
	Unnamed	1/12	M	W		TN
Evans,	Margaret	62	F	W	Farmer	NC
	Hannah	19	F	W		TN

1860 Fentress Co. TN Census

Name		Age Remarks	Sex	Race	Profession	Birth Place

Civil District No. 7
Recorded 11 July 1860

Name		Age Remarks	Sex	Race	Profession	Birth Place
Riley,	Alexander	36	M	W	Farmer	TN
	Sarah	36	F	W		TN
	Thomas Jr.	18	M	W	Farmer	TN
	Nancy	16	F	W		TN
	William	4	M	W		TN
	James	1	M	W		TN
Rich,	Calvin	23	M	W	Farmer	TN
	Margaret	21	F	W		TN
	Mary	3	F	W		TN
	Thomas	1/12	M	W		TN
Richardson,	Thomas	5?	M	W	Day Laborer	TN
	Anna	47	M	W		TN
	Angeline	22	F	W		TN
	Hariot	20	F	W		TN
	Martha	18	F	W		TN
	Martin	15	M	W	Day Laborer	TN
Livingston,	Henry	28	M	W	Blacksmith	TN
	Lucinda	22	F	W		TN
	Lean	4	F	W		TN
	James T.	3	M	W		TN
	Robert E.	10/12	M	W		TN
Riley,	Thomas	57	M	W	Farmer	VA
	Sarah	52	F	W		TN
	Eliza J.	23	F	W		TN
	Hariot	21	F	W		TN
	Elizabeth	18	F	W		TN
	John B.	9	M	W		TN
	Amanda	6	F	W		TN
	Mary	12	F	W		TN
	Nancy	77	F	W	No Occupation	VA
Huff,	A. J.	24	M	W	Mill Wright	TN
	Nancy	19	F	W		TN
	Sophronia	1	F	W		TN

1860 Fentress Co. TN Census

Name		Age Remarks	Sex	Race	Profession	Birth Place

Civil District No. 7
Recorded 11 July 1860

Name		Age	Sex	Race	Profession	Birth Place
Williams,	H. B.	39	M	W	Farmer	TN
	Rebeccah	50	F	W		KY
Burton,	W. R. F.	22	M	W	Leader School	TN
	Tamzin A.	20	F	W		TN
	Josephine	8	F	W		TN

Recorded 12 July 1860

Name		Age	Sex	Race	Profession	Birth Place
Pile,	Levi	36	M	W	Day Laborer	TN
	Anna	38	F	W		TN
	Pleasant	16	M	W	Day Laborer	TN
	Mary C.	9	F	W		TN
	R? J.	8	F	W		TN
	James D.	3	M	W		TN
William,	Theophalus	47	M	W	Farmer	NC
	Cinthia	49	F	W		TN
	Elizabeth	25	F	W		TN
	John	23	M	W		TN
	Artemia	20	F	W		TN
	James H.	18	M	W	Farmer	TN
	Martha	16	F	W		TN
	Francis M.	13	M	W		TN
	Pleasant	11	M	W		TN
	William H.	8	M	W		TN
	Bernetta	6	F	W		TN
	Thetney	3	F	W		TN
Sherman,	Willet	32	M	W	Mechanic	VA
Rich,	William	72	M	W	Farmer	NC
	Milly	44	F	W		KY
	Catharine	18	F	W		TN
	Jacob M.	11	M	W		TN
	William J.	9	M	W		TN
	Eliza L.	6	F	W		TN
	Thomas A. W.	2	M	W		TN

1860 Fentress Co. TN Census

Name		Age Remarks	Sex	Race	Profession	Birth Place

Civil District No. 7
Recorded 12 July 1860

Name		Age	Sex	Race	Profession	Birth Place
Crouch,	E. H.	33	M	W	Farmer	TN
	Sarah	23	F	W		TN
	Rebeccah J.	7	F	W		TN
	Alama	5	F	W		TN
	William H.	1	M	W		TN
Crouch,	George W.	27	M	W	Tenant	TN
	Lucinda A.	24	F	W		TN
	James A.	8	M	W		TN
	John W.	6	M	W		TN
	Timothy C.	4	M	W		TN
	Margaret L.	2	F	W		TN
Dishman,	Archibald	53	M	W	Farmer	NC
	Jane	55	F	W		KY
	Milly	24	F	W		TN
	Anthew	23	M	W	Farmer	TN
	Lewis	21	M	W	Farmer	TN
	Thomas C.	16	M	W	Farmer	TN
	James	13	M	W		TN
Dishman,	Jefferson	28	M	W	Farmer	TN
	Mary	32	F	W		TN
	Margaret	5	F	W		TN
	Clarinda C.	3	F	W		TN
	Archabald	3/12	M	W		TN
Smith,	Mary	47	F	W	Day Laborer	KY
	Srepte	19	F	W		KY
	Melinda	13	F	W		KY
	Emeline	3	F	W		TN
	Electa	1	F	W		TN
Key,	John	31	M	W	Day Laborer	TN
	Mary	47	F	W		VA
	James W.	12	M	W		TN
	Lean	10	F	W		TN
	Martha	7	F	W		TN
Rigney,	John C.	20	M	W	Day Laborer	TN
	Levina	19	F	W		TN

1860 Fentress Co. TN Census

Name		Age Remarks	Sex	Race	Profession	Birth Place

Civil District No. 7
Recorded 12 July 1860

Name		Age	Sex	Race	Profession	Birth Place
Manard,	Cade	27	M	W	Tenant	TN
	Martha	27	F	W		TN
	Sarah J.	3	F	W		TN
	Wayman	3/12	M	W		TN
Jones,	James S.	43	M	W	Tenant	KY
	Sarah	39	F	W		TN
	William H.	23	M	W	Tenant	TN
	Henry F.	18	M	W	Tenant	TN
	Thomas J.	15	M	W	Tenant	TN
	John	13	M	W		TN
	James H.	11	M	W		TN
	Philip	8	M	W		TN
	Jesse	7	M	W		TN
	Calvin	5	M	W		TN
	Mary	3	F	W		TN
Rigney,	Griffy	75	M	W	No Occupation	VA
	Levina	75	F	W		VA
	Jeremiah	13	M	W		TN
	Perry	11	M	W		TN
Birk,	Thomas	77	M	W	Farmer	VA
	Mary	62	F	W		TN
	Mary	24	F	W		TN
	Henry	21	M	W		TN
	Ibey	17	F	W		KY
	Barbara A.	3	F	W		TN
Young,	Robert	32	M	W	Farmer	KY
	Susan	25	F	W		TN
	Matilda	13	F	W		KY
	Andrew J.	10	M	W		KY
	Melissa C.	8	F	W		KY
	Mary A.	6	F	W		KY
	George M. D.	4	M	W		TN
Craig,	Mahala	47	F	W	Domestic	KY
	Eli	24	M	W	Herdsman	TN

Name		Age Remarks	Sex	Race	Profession	Birth Place
Craig,	Goldman	33	M	W	Tenant	TN
	Permela	28	F	W		TN
	John	11	M	W		TN
	Henry	9	M	W		TN
	James	8	M	W		KY
	Dalilah J.	7	F	W		TN
	Adibid	3	F	W		TN
	Unnamed	1/12	F	W		TN
Harmon,	Caleb	60	F	W	Tenant	VA
	Mahala	24	F	W		KY
	Rebecca	21	F	W		KY
	James	19	M	W		KY

Recorded 13 July 1860

Name		Age Remarks	Sex	Race	Profession	Birth Place
?troris,	David C.	39	M	W		TN
	Melissa	39	F	W		TN
	Mary J.	17	F	W		KY
	Sarah A.	15	F	W		TN
	James T.	12	M	W		TN
	Artemia E.	9	F	W		TN
	Joel R.	6	M	W		TN
	Matilda E.	3	F	W		TN
Evans,	Elisha	39	M	W	Tenant	KY
	Sarah	39	F	W		TN
	Amanda	1?	F	W		TN
	John M.	12	M	W		TN
	Thetney	10	F	W		KY
	Wm. W.	9	M	W		KY
	Jefferson	8	M	W		TN
	Mary J.	5	F	W		TN
	Sarah A.	3	F	W		TN
	James H.	2	M	W		TN
	Elizabeth	6/12	F	W		TN

1860 Fentress Co. TN Census

Name		Age Remarks	Sex	Race	Profession	Birth Place

Civil District No. 7
Recorded 13 July 1860

Name		Age	Sex	Race	Profession	Birth Place
Rigney,	Bluford	35	M	W	Farmer	TN
	Ann G.	22	F	W		TN
	James	21	M	W	Farmer	TN
	Henry	17	M	W	Farmer	TN
	Louisa	15	F	W		TN
	Washington	14	M	W		TN
	Matilda	12	F	W		TN
	Mork	8	F	W		TN
	William	1	M	W		TN
Young,	Susan	50	F	W	Tenant	NC
	Lily	27	F	W		TN
	William	24	M	W	Tenant	KY
	John	21	M	W	Tenant	TN
	Eda	18	F	W		TN
	James	16	M	W	Tenant	TN
	Martha	15	F	W		TN
	George W.	5	M	W		TN
Shelton,	John	56	M	W	Farmer	NC
	Sarah	37	F	W		TN
	Lucinda	21	F	W		TN
	Anna	20	F	W		KY
	Martha J.	18	F	W		TN
	William J.	16	M	W	Farmer	TN
	Sarah A. E.	14	F	W		TN
	John E.	12	M	W		TN
	George W.	11	M	W		TN
	Ruben	9	M	W		TN
	James C.	7	M	W		TN
	Martin V.	4	M	W		TN
Rigney,	Harrison	21	M	W	Tenant	TN
	Matilda	23	F	W		TN
	Sarah A. E.	3/12	F	W		TN
Jones,	Eli	23	M	W	Tenant	TN
	Martha A.	21	F	W		TN

1860 Fentress Co. TN Census

Name		Age Remarks	Sex	Race	Profession	Birth Place

Name		Age	Sex	Race	Profession	Birth Place
Smith,	John C.	64	M	W	Farmer	NC
	Margaret	47	F	W		TN
	Electa A.	14	F	W		TN
	Luther T.	13	M	W		TN
	David C.	11	M	W		TN
	Shery A.	9	M	W		TN
	William J.	5	M	W		TN
	Flonna	3	F	W		TN
Lawhorn,	Jesse	48	M	W	Farmer	VA
	Manerva	40	F	W		TN
	Chestanna	17	M	W	Farmer	TN
	Franklin	12	M	W		TN
	Virginia	9	F	W		TN
	Lucinda	6	F	W		TN
	Tennesse	9/12	F	W		TN
Davidson,	B. R.	47	M	W	Farmer	TN
	Judith	42	F	W		TN
	Eliza A.	15	F	W		TN
	Manerva J.	13	F	W		TN
	Martin B.	11	M	W		TN
	Albert G.	7	M	W		TN
Daniel,	Mary	20	F	W	Domestic	TN
Harrison,	Marion	15	M	W	Farmer	TN
Davidson,	Pearson H.	38	M	W	Farmer	TN
	Matilda	29	F	W		TN
	George A.	7	M	W		TN
	William B.	6	M	W		TN
	Benjamin L.	4	M	W		TN
	Martha L.	3	F	W		TN
	Unnamed	1	M	W		TN
Davidson,	Lucinda	69	F	W	Tenant	KY
	Eliza	25	F	W		TN

1860 Fentress Co. TN Census

Name		Age Remarks	Sex	Race	Profession	Birth Place

Civil District No. 7
Recorded 13 July 1860

Name		Age	Sex	Race	Profession	Birth Place
Roger,	Anderson	40	M	W	Farmer	KY
	Agnes	40	F	W		TN
	Mary A.	19	F	W		TN
	Thomas	16	M	W	Farmer	TN
	Elijah	14	M	W		TN
	John	12	M	W		TN
	William	10	M	W		TN
	Lois S.	7	F	W		TN
	James C.	6	M	W		TN
	Vianna	3	F	W		TN
	George A. C.	1	M	W		TN
Rencan,	Christian	55	M	W	Farmer	TN
	Margaret	32	F	W		TN
	Jane	28	F	W		TN
	Martha	25	F	W		TN
	Elizabeth	21	F	W		TN
	Roland	19	M	W	Farmer	TN
	James	12	M	W		TN
	Elizabeth	54	F	W		TN
Honey,	John	26	M	W		TN
	Ruthy	31	F	W		TN
	Mary J.	2	F	W		TN
Davidson,	Archabald	49	M	W	Tenant	TN
	Emeline	42	F	W		VA
	Martha	13	F	W		TN
	John	10	M	W		TN
	Sarah P.	9	F	W		TN
	William T.	7	M	W		TN
	Mary M.	5	F	W		TN
	Ruthy R.	2	F	W		KY
	Rebeccah E.	8/12	F	W		TN

1860 Fentress Co. TN Census

Name		Age Remarks	Sex	Race	Profession	Birth Place

Name		Age	Sex	Race	Profession	Birth Place
Hicks,	John	30	M	W	Carpenter	TN
	Ellen J.	28	F	W		TN
	Haydon	11	M	W		TN
	Mary A.	10	F	W		TN
	Woolsey	8	M	W		TN
	Robert	7	M	W		TN
	Sarah M.	6	F	W		TN
	Adelaice	4	F	W		TN
	Margaret	5/12	F	W		TN
Upchurch,	James	35	M	W	Tenant	KY
	Elizabeth	30	F	W		TN
	Lucinda	13	F	W		KY
	Sevina	11	F	W		KY
	John T.	9	M	W		TN
	William J.	6	M	W		TN
	Sarah C.	9/12	F	W		TN
Rayn,	C. B.	30	M	W	Merchant	KY
	Adilvice	22	F	W		KY
	Mattie	5	F	W		TN
	Florence	3	F	W		TN
	Pauline	9/12	F	W		TN
Hay,	A. A.	19	M	W	Salesman	KY
Cummings,	Rebeccah	24	F	W	Domestic	TN
Davidson,	Wm. A.	46	M	W	Farmer	TN
	Margaret	41	F	W		KY
	John B.	11	M	W		KY
	Robert	9	M	W		TN
	Leann	3	F	W		TN
	Edward	1	M	W		TN
Upchurch,	T. W.	28	M	W	Farmer	TN
	Sarah A.	25	F	W		KY
	Lucinda J.	4	F	W		TN
	Sarah E.	10/12	F	W		TN

1860 Fentress Co. TN Census

Name		Age Remarks	Sex	Race	Profession	Birth Place

Civil District No. 7
Recorded 14 July 1860

Name		Age	Sex	Race	Profession	Birth Place
Davidson,	Stephen	43	M	W	Wagon Maker	TN
	Amanda	30	F	W		TN
	Lucinda M.	11	F	W		TN
	William	9	M	W		TN
	Rebeccah E.	8	F	W		TN
	Jonathan F.	4	M	W		TN
	Henry W. F.	2	M	W		TN
Davidson,	Samuel R.	31	M	W	Farmer	TN
	Sarah	34	F	W	Domestic	TN
	Martha	14	F	W	Domestic	TN
Francis,	H. W.	29	M	W	Cabinet Maker	TN
	D. M.	28	F	W		TN
Evans,	Rebeccah	66	F	W	Domestic	TN
Rule,	Jefferson	27	M	W	Tenant	TN
	Louisa	24	F	W		TN
	Eliza	5	F	W		KY
	John W. M.	2	M	W		TN
Brown,	William	32	M	W	Farmer	KY
	Ania	34	F	W		TN
	Mary E.	9	F	W		KY
	James R.	7	M	W		TN
	David T.	5	M	W		TN
	Serilda J.	2	F	W		TN
Young,	Burdon	12	M	W		KY
Travis,	William	77	M	W	Farmer	MD
	Mary	72	F	W		TN
	Rose	75	F	B		?
Richardson,	Robert	76	M	W	Farmer	VA
	Thetney	56	F	W		TN
	Mitchel	21	M	W	Farmer	TN
	Hiram	18	M	W	Farmer	TN
Westmoreland,	Stephen	42	M	W	Farmer	TN
	Tabitha	46	F	W		TN
	Emeline C.	14	F	W		KY
	Martha J.	9	F	W		TN

1860 Fentress Co. TN Census

Name		Age Remarks	Sex	Race	Profession	Birth Place

Civil District No. 7
Recorded 14 July 1860

Name		Age	Sex	Race	Profession	Birth Place
Edwards,	Dice	37	F	W	Farming	TN
	Vinson	20	M	W	Farming	TN
	Richard S.	17	M	W	Farming	TN
	Sarah A.	15	F	W		TN
	Arther	13	M	W		TN
	Stephen H.	10	M	W		TN
	Mary A. T.	3	F	W		TN
Rains,	William	23	M	W	Farmer	KY
	Sarah A.	21	F	W		TN
	Mary A.	4	F	W		TN
	Isaac S.	3	M	W		TN
	George W.	1	M	W		TN
Rich,	John	25	M	W	Tenant	TN
	Mary	23	F	W		TN
	Martha J.	1	F	W		TN

1860 Fentress Co. TN Census

Name		Age Remarks	Sex	Race	Profession	Birth Place

Civil District No. 8
Recorded 16 July 1860

Name		Age	Sex	Race	Profession	Birth Place
Cummings,	Milly	46	F	W	Domestic	TN
	William F.	20	M	W	Day Laborer	KY
	Charlotte	17	F	W		KY
	Nancy E.	13	F	W		KY
	Charlotte	17	F	W		KY
	Nancy E.	13	F	W		KY
	Louisa	10	F	W		KY
Upchurch,	Joseph	59	M	W	Farmer	NC
	Jane	54	F	W		KY
	Avery G.	16	M	W		TN
	Elias H.	12	M	W		TN
Upchurch,	John J.	21	M	W	Tenant	TN
	Sarah	21	F	W		TN
	William J.	1	M	W		TN
Crabtree,	Ephraim	30	M	W	Farmer	TN
	Lucinda	30	F	W		KY
	Martin	10	M	W		TN
	Jane	7	F	W		TN
	Naoma	4	F	W		TN
	Dorcas	1	F	W		TN
Hatfield,	Ephraim	73	M	W	Farmer	TN
	Dorcas	63	F	W		TN
Pile,	Conrad	45	M	W	Farmer	TN
	Susanah	45	F	W		TN
	Sherrod	14	M	W		TN
	James	13	M	W		TN
	William	11	M	W		TN
	Washington	8	M	W		TN
	Floyd	6	M	W		TN
Rich,	John	36	M	W	Tenant	TN
	Lucinda A.	30	F	W		TN
Upchurch,	Sevena	11	F	W		KY

1860 Fentress Co. TN Census

Name		Age Remarks	Sex	Race	Profession	Birth Place

Civil District No. 8
Recorded 16 July 1860

Name		Age	Sex	Race	Profession	Birth Place
Pile,	John C.	58	M	W	Farmer	TN
	Nancy	52	F	W		KY
	William	23	M	W		TN
	Elizabeth	18	F	W		TN
	Martha	16	F	W		TN
	James	13	M	W		TN
	Louisa	10	F	W		TN
	Lucinda	6	F	W		TN
Williams,	William B.	45	M	W	Farmer	NC
	Susanah	42	F	W		TN
	William F.	22	M	W		TN
	Milly	20	F	W		TN
	Elijah	19	M	W		TN
	Alexander	15	M	W		TN
	Absolum	13	M	W		TN
	Rebeccah	11	F	W		TN
Williams,	?	18	M	W	Tenant	TN
	Elizabeth	17	F	W		TN
	Flemington	11/12	M	W		TN
Williams,	Francis	70	M	W	Farmer	NC
	Milly	70	F	W		NC
	Mary	26	F	W		TN
	Francis A.	4	M	W		TN
Williams,	William	23	M	W	Tenant	TN
	Lucinda	20	F	W		TN
	Melvin A.	2	M	W		TN
	Oliver J.	1	M	W		TN
Pile,	Elijah	65	M	W	Farmer	NC
	Rebeccah	63	F	W		NC
	Mary	29	F	W		TN
	Nancy	23	F	W		TN
Overton,	Dalia	28	M	W	Day Laborer	TN
McFarlin,	Sarah	12	F	W		TN

1860 Fentress Co. TN Census

Name		Age Remarks	Sex	Race	Profession	Birth Place

Civil District No. 8
Recorded 16 July 1860

Name		Age	Sex	Race	Profession	Birth Place
Pile,	Jefferson A.	32	M	W	Tenant	TN
	Sarah J.	30	F	W		TN
	Benjamin D.	6	M	W		TN
	Thomas	3	M	W		TN
Pile,	William Jr.	44	M	W	Farmer	TN
	Mary	43	F	W		TN
	Stephen	21	M	W		TN
	Nancy	19	F	W		TN
	John W.	17	M	W		TN
	Jefferson	14	M	W		TN
	James	13	M	W		TN
	Balaam	9	M	W		TN
	Lavina	7	F	W		TN
	William B.	5	M	W		TN
	Alice	1	F	W		TN
Pile,	Pleasant D.	26	M	W	Tenant	TN
	Aley	25	F	W		KY
	Emeline	8	F	W		TN
	Rebeccah	6	F	W		TN
	Wilson	4	M	W		TN
	Mary J.	1	F	W		TN
Gregory,	John	25	M	W	Tenant	KY
	Melissa	25	F	W		TN
Rich,	Mary	6	F	W		TN
Latham,	C. W.	58	M	W	Tenant	TN
	James	30	M	W	Tenant	TN
	Lafayette	27	M	W	Tenant	TN
	Louisa	21	F	W		TN
	Fanny	18	F	W		TN
	Martha	14	F	W		TN
Burton,	Marion	28	M	W		TN
	Nancy	24	F	W		TN

1860 Fentress Co. TN Census

Name		Age Remarks	Sex	Race	Profession	Birth Place

Civil District No. 8
Recorded 16 July 1860

Name		Age	Sex	Race	Profession	Birth Place
Johns,	Eli	53	M	W	Farmer	TN
	Chestess?	26	F	W		TN
	Emma T.	9	F	W		TN
	William L.	8	M	W		TN
	Lydia E.	6	F	W		TN
	Martha L.	5	F	W		TN
	Joseph W.	4	M	W		TN
	Doctor F.	1	M	W		TN
	Unnamed	5/12	M	W		TN
Price,	Nathaniel	38	M	W	Tenant	TN
	Jane	46	F	W		TN
	Anna M.	6	F	W		TN
Crouch,	James	37	M	W	Farmer	TN
	Lucy L.	31	F	W		TN
	John	14	M	W		TN
	Martin	12	M	W		TN
	James	10	M	W		TN
	Elizabeth	8	F	W		TN
	Miram	6	F	W		TN
	Deborah	4	F	W		TN
	Samuel	2	M	W		TN
Williams,	John	39	M	W	Farmer	TN
	Jane	25	F	W		TN
	Mary	13	F	W		TN
	Levina J.	11	F	W		TN
	James	6	M	W		TN
	Unnamed	2/12	F	W		TN
Cail,	Elizabeth	38	F	W	Domestic	TN
	Elizabeth	18	F	W	Domestic	TN
	John	15	M	W	Farmer	TN

Recorded 17 July 1860

Name		Age	Sex	Race	Profession	Birth Place
Wood,	Jonathan E.	29	M	W	Tenant	TN
	Jane	23	F	W		TN
	Vestina	2	F	W		TN
	Mary J. E.	9/12	F	W		TN

1860 Fentress Co. TN Census

Name		Age Remarks	Sex	Race	Profession	Birth Place

Civil District No. 8
Recorded 17 July 1860

Name		Age Remarks	Sex	Race	Profession	Birth Place
Kidd,	James	37	M	W	Farmer	KY
	Martha	31	F	W		TN
	Rebeccah E.	12	F	W		TN
	Mary J.	10	F	W		TN
	Sarah C.	5	F	W		TN
	Phebe A.	4	F	W		TN
	Miva M.	3	F	W		TN
	George W.	14 days	M	W		TN
West,	John	39	M	W	Farmer	TN
	Jane	39	F	W		TN
	William	20	M	W	Farmer	TN
	Elizabeth	17	F	W		TN
	Mary A.	14	F	W		TN
	John J.	11	M	W		TN
	Tilman	7	M	W		TN
	Lucinda	2	F	W		TN
Frogge,	John W.	30	M	W	Farmer	TN
	Nancy	36	F	W		TN
	Deborah	9	F	W		TN
	Penigh	8	F	W		TN
	Timothy	6	M	W		TN
	James	4	M	W		TN
	Cynel	2	M	W		TN
	Deborah	56	F	W	Domestic	TN
	Rebeccah	22	F	W	Domestic	TN
	Mary	19	F	W		TN
West,	James	22	M	W	Day Laborer	TN
	Sarah	20	F	W		KY
	Timothy	3	M	W		TN
	Mary	5/12	F	W		TN
Crabtree,	George W.	27	M	W	Farmer	TN
	Nancy	26	F	W		TN

104

1860 Fentress Co. TN Census

Name		Age Remarks	Sex	Race	Profession	Birth Place

Civil District No. 8
Recorded 17 July 1860

Name		Age	Sex	Race	Profession	Birth Place
Gennings,	Mark	53	M	W	Farmer	KY
	Anna	48	F	W		TN
	Rhoda	19	F	W		TN
	John G.	12	F	W		TN
	Melissa M.	7	F	W		TN
Rilley,	William	32	M	W	Tenant	TN
	Elizabeth	42	F	W		TN
	Eliza A.	17	F	W		KY
	Thomas M.	13	M	W		KY
	Ranson	11	M	W		TN
	Martha J.	9	F	W		TN
	Ambrose B.	8	M	W		TN
	Susan	6	F	W		TN
	Maiad S.	4	M	W		TN
	Rebeccah B.	2	F	W		TN
Pruitt,	John	70	M	W	Tenant	VA
	Susan	56	F	W		VA
	Jane	25	F	W		TN
	Stasia	22	F	W		TN
	John	8	M	W		KY
	Rebeccah	6	F	W		KY
Johnson,	William	25	M	W	Day Laborer	TN
	Mary	24	F	W		TN
	Elizabeth	1	F	W		TN
Pile,	John I.	36	M	W	Farmer	TN
	Elsey	40	F	W		TN
	James F.	14	M	W		TN
	William J.	13	M	W		TN
	Elijah N.	11	M	W		TN
	Mary J.	9	F	W		TN
	John C.	6	M	W		TN
	Absolam B.	5	M	W		TN
	Tabitha C.	1	F	W		TN

1860 Fentress Co. TN Census

Name		Age Remarks	Sex	Race	Profession	Birth Place

Civil District No. 8
Recorded 17 July 1860

Name		Age Remarks	Sex	Race	Profession	Birth Place
Gennings,	Anthony	53	M	W	Tenant	KY
	Martha	38	F	W		NC
	Nancy	14	F	W		TN
	John	11	M	W		TN
	Sarah C.	5	F	W		KY
	Wm. E.	3	M	W		KY
	Sherrod W.	4/12	M	W		TN
Evans,	James L.	39	M	W	Tenant	TN
	Eliza	38	F	W		KY
	John	18	M	W		TN
	William	15	M	W	Tenant	TN
	Amanda	13	F	W		TN
	Sarah A.	11	F	W		TN
	Margaret	7	F	W		TN
	Cornilius F.	1	M	W		TN
Kidd,	Margaret	64	F	W	Domestic	VA
Delk,	John	41	M	W	Farmer	TN
	Sarah	37	F	W		TN
	Wm.	17	M	W		TN
	Sherrod	16	M	W	Farmer	TN
	Philip	14	M	W	Farmer	TN
	Mary	12	F	W		TN
	Dudley	10	M	W		TN
	Elizabeth	7	F	W		TN
	Ellis	5	M	W		TN
	Jasper	4	M	W		TN
	John	2	M	W		TN
	Lucinda	5/12	F	W		TN
Shepherd,	Levi	32	M	W	Cabinet Maker	KY
	Martha J.	28	F	W		TN
	Wm. W.	7	M	W		TN
	James M.	5	M	W		TN
	Nimrod E.	3	M	W		TN
	Janvina J.	3	F	W		TN
	Lucinda A.	9/12	F	W		TN

1860 Fentress Co. TN Census

Name		Age Remarks	Sex	Race	Profession	Birth Place

Civil District No. 8
Recorded 17 July 1860

Name		Age	Sex	Race	Profession	Birth Place
Latham,	Martha	38	F	W	Farming	TN
	John W.	12	M	W		TN
	Calvin L.	7	M	W		TN
	Mary E.	5	F	W		TN
Adkins,	Martha E.	22	F	W	Domestic	TN
	James	2	M	W		KY
Young,	Lucinda	45	F	W	Tenant	TN
	Sampson	29	M	W	Tenant	TN
	Hannah E.	20	F	W		TN
Duncan,	Burton M.	28	M	W	Farmer	TN
	Emeline J.	25	F	W		TN
Neal,	Vestina	5	F	W		TN
Duncan,	Sampson W.	3	M	W		TN
	Martha E.	1	F	W		TN

Recorded 18 July 1860

Name		Age	Sex	Race	Profession	Birth Place
Redmon,	James R.	26	M	W	Tenant	TN
	Margaret	24	F	W		TN
Rhodes,	John	89	M	W	Farmer	SC
	Elizabeth	49	F	W		KY
Adkinson,	Mary W.	24	F	W	Domestic	TN
Blakely,	Wm. C.	15	M	W	Farmer	TN
Adkinson,	Wiley E.	5	M	W		TN
	Wm. D.	1	M	W		TN
Delk,	David	42	M	W	Farmer	TN
	Sarah S.	38	F	W		TN
	Lemml	19	M	W	Farmer	TN
	Jeremiah	16	M	W	Farmer	TN
	Emeline A.	15	F	W		TN
	Martha	12	F	W		TN
	Fruly	10	F	W		TN
	Edley P.	8	M	W		TN
	David Jr.	6	M	W		TN
	Amanda L.	4	F	W		TN
	Delilah	2	F	W		TN

1860 Fentress Co. TN Census

Name		Age Remarks	Sex	Race	Profession	Birth Place

Civil District No. 8
Recorded 18 July 1860

Name		Age	Sex	Race	Profession	Birth Place
Pile,	William Sr.	50	M	W	Farmer	TN
	Mary	43	F	W		TN
	Priscilla	21	F	W		TN
	Martha	18	F	W		TN
	Alvin	16	M	W	Farmer	TN
	Mary	15	F	W		TN
	Levina	13	F	W		TN
	Eliza	11	F	W		TN
	Delpha	8	F	W		TN
	Attah	2	F	W		TN
	Jasper	7/12	M	W		TN
Miller,	Artemius D.	45	F	W	Farming	KY
	William P.	24	M	W	School Leader	TN
	Permelia A.	21	F	W		TN
	Josiah A.	18	M	W	Farmer	TN
	Pleasant J.	15	M	W	Farmer	TN
	John I.	12	M	W		TN
	?Pounqulla L.	7	F	W		TN
Redman,	Francis	73	M	W	Farmer	NC
	Susanah	71	F	W		VA
Crouch,	Martin	61	M	W	Farmer	KY
	Oliva	46	F	W		KY
	Vianna	18	F	W		TN
	Lucinda	16	F	W		TN
	Elizabeth	14	F	W		TN
	Pleasant D.	12	M	W		TN
	Julia A.	11	F	W		TN
	Mary E.	9	F	W		TN
	Caroline	7	F	W		TN
	Mary	5	F	W		TN
	Granville M.	2	M	W		TN
Renean,	William	24	M	W	Day Laborer	TN
	Jane	18	F	W		TN
Crouch,	William	62	M	W	Farmer	VA
	Elizabeth	61	F	W		VA
	Martania	11	F	W		TN

1860 Fentress Co. TN Census

Name		Age Remarks	Sex	Race	Profession	Birth Place

Civil District No. 8
Recorded 18 July 1860

Name		Age Remarks	Sex	Race	Profession	Birth Place
Williams,	John	66	M	W	Farmer	NC
	Levina	63	F	W		NC
Crabtree,	Stekly	25	M	W	Tenant	TN
	Eliza	24	F	W		TN
	Margaret J.	2	F	W		TN
	Sarah A.	10/12	F	W		TN
Hatfield,	Berry	44	M	W	Tenant	KY
	Elsey	45	F	W		TN
	Robert	22	M	W	Tenant	TN
	Francis	16	M	W	Tenant	TN
	Nancy	13	F	W		TN
	Wm. N.	11	M	W		TN
	Jesse V.	7	M	W		TN
Helks,	Alfred	29	M	W	Tenant	TN
	Lucinda E.	8	F	W		TN
	Luvernia	2	F	W		TN
Huff,	Alexander	57	M	W	Farmer	KY
	Martha	39	F	W		KY
	Preston	18	M	W		KY
	Lucinda	16	F	W		KY
	John	14	M	W		KY
	McKager P.	12	F	W		KY
	Landan C. H.	10	M	W		KY
	Mary C.	8	F	W		KY
	James H.	7	M	W		KY
	Thursa J.	5	F	W		KY
	Elander E.	3	F	W		KY
	Alexander C.	2	M	W		KY
	Jackson	25	M	W	Day Laborer	KY

1860 Fentress Co. TN Census

Name		Age Remarks	Sex	Race	Profession	Birth Place

Civil District No. 8
Recorded 19 July 1860

Name		Age	Sex	Race	Profession	Birth Place
Evans,	Charlotte	36	F	W	Gardening	TN
	James H.	12	M	W		TN
	John	11	M	W		TN
	Margaret J.	9	F	W		TN
	Drury	8	M	W		TN
	Pleasant C.	7	M	W		TN
	Osca	1	M	W		TN
Crabtree,	Hiram	42	M	W	Farmer	TN
	Manervia	38	F	W		TN
	Thomas	19	M	W	Farmer	TN
	Anza	18	M	W	Farmer	TN
	Nancy	15	F	W		TN
	Mary J. E.	8	F	W		TN
	Winnie	6	F	W		TN
Sampson,	Isham	48	M	W	Farmer Tenant	KY
	Elizabeth	39	F	W		KY
	Abner	14	M	W		TN
	Martha	12	F	W		TN
	Mira	9	F	W		TN
	Missoanie A.	7	F	W		TN
	Giles	5	M	W		TN
	William	3	M	W		TN
	Hisam	7/12	M	W		TN
Frogge,	Lucisa	46	F	W	Tenant	KY
	Mary A.	21	F	W		TN
	S. A. J.	17	M	W	Tenant	TN
	Jane T.	16	F	W		TN
	Rachel J.	13	F	W		TN
	Margaret J.	7	F	W		TN
Craig,	Elizabeth	53	F	W	Day Laborer	KY
	James S.	18	M	W	Day Laborer	KY

1860 Fentress Co. TN Census

Name		Age Remarks	Sex	Race	Profession	Birth Place

Civil District No. 8
Recorded 19 July 1860

Name		Age	Sex	Race	Profession	Birth Place
Crabtree,	James	52	M	W	Tenant	TN
	Nancy	42	F	W		TN
	Alexander	18	M	W	Tenant	TN
	William	16	M	W	Tenant	TN
	Alvin	13	M	W		TN
	Pernetta	11	F	W		TN
	Sarah J.	8	F	W		TN
Gray,	Robert V.	36	M	W	Farmer	TN
	Emeline A.	28	F	W		TN
	Mary E.	9	F	W		TN
	Nebraska	5	F	W		TN
	Sarah R.	4	F	W		TN
	Josephine	2	F	W		TN
Miller,	Pleasant	51	M	W	Farmer	KY
	Sarah	40	F	W		KY
	Tennessee	17	F	W		TN
	Caroline	15	F	W		TN
	Mary	14	F	W		TN
	Nancy	11	F	W		TN
	John M.	9	M	W		TN
	Evavina	6	F	W		TN
	Fatina	4	F	W		TN
	Lucy	10/12	F	W		TN
Miller,	William	46	M	W	Farmer	KY
	Martha	34	F	W		KY
	James B. S.	12	M	W		TN
	Aliravine?	11	M	W		TN
	Lean E.	8	F	W		TN
	Alice G.	3	F	W		TN
Richardson,	D. N.	30	M	W	Farmer	TN
	Angeline D.	29	F	W		TN
	Lila A.	6	F	W		TN
	John J.	4	M	W		TN
	Elbridge N.	2	M	W		TN
	Abigail	76	F	W		VA

1860 Fentress Co. TN Census

Name		Age Remarks	Sex	Race	Profession	Birth Place

Civil District No. 8
Recorded 19 July 1860

Name		Age	Sex	Race	Profession	Birth Place
Huff,	John	75	M	W	Farmer	VA
	Serena	45	F	W		KY
	Bransford	9	M	W		TN
	Florence	5	F	W		TN
	Dion	1	F	W		TN
Huff,	Clarborne	47	M	W	Farmer	TN
	Serilde	36	F	W		KY
	Alvin	17	M	W	Farmer	TN
Rich,	Rouse	15	M	W	Farmer	TN
Miller,	Pearson	88	M	W	Farmer	VA
	James	41	M	W	Farmer	TN
Rains,	Mriah	81	M	W	No Occupation	VA
Miller,	Amstia	44	M	W	Farmer	TN
	Mary	43	F	W		TN
	Martenia	16	F	W		TN
	Alvin	14	M	W		TN
	Erman	12	F	W		TN
	Hugh	10	M	W		TN
McFarland,	Harrison J.	27	M	W	Tenant	TN
	Sarah J.	22	F	W		TN
	Jackson Y.	5	M	W		TN
	Lucy E.	3	F	W		TN
	Delia A.	3/12	F	W		TN
Delk,	James	27	M	W	Farmer	TN
	Matilda	27	F	W		TN
	Pamela J.	7	F	W		TN
	Columbus J.	5	M	W		TN
	John M.	2	M	W		TN
	James A.	1	M	W		TN
Stewart,	Robert	25	M	W	Day Laborer	TN

1860 Fentress Co. TN Census

Name		Age Remarks	Sex	Race	Profession	Birth Place

Civil District No. 8
Recorded 20 July 1860

Name		Age	Sex	Race	Profession	Birth Place
Morgan,	William	53	M	W	Tenant	TN
	Genetta	36	F	W		NC
	Hannah	19	F	W		TN
	John W.	14	M	W	Tenant	TN
	Matilda	11	F	W		TN
	Lyia	11	F	W		TN
	James	8	M	W		TN
	Hulda	7	F	W		TN
	Henry	5	M	W		TN
	Granville	1	M	W		TN
	Stokely	3/12	M	W		TN
McGinnis,	Andrew	59	M	W	Farmer	TN
	Nancy	50	F	W		TN
	Hamelton	21	M	W	Farmer	TN
	Juitt	19	M	W	Farmer	TN
	Fliming	17	M	W	Farmer	TN
	Andrew	10	M	W		TN
Rains,	James	35	M	W	Farmer	KY
	Granville	22	M	W	Farmer	KY
McGinnis,	Archabald	24	M	W	Tenant	TN
	Luvinah	18	F	W		TN
	Mary	22	F	W		TN
	Henderson	21	M	W	Tenant	TN
	Nancy	19	F	W		TN
	Laticia	17	F	W		TN
	Noble	15	M	W	Tenant	TN
	Manersia	13	F	W		TN
	Martha	12	F	W		TN
	Susan	10	F	W		TN
Simpson,	John	60	M	W	Farmer	VA
	Sarah	53	F	W		OH
	Lavina	17	F	W		TN
	Tehrisa	15	F	W		TN
	John	11	M	W		TN
	William D.	9	M	W		TN

1860 Fentress Co. TN Census

Name		Age Remarks	Sex	Race	Profession	Birth Place

Civil District No. 8
Recorded 20 July 1860

Name		Age	Sex	Race	Profession	Birth Place
Guffer,	Harrison	30	M	W	Farmer	TN
	Parlee	22	F	W		TN
	William D.	5	M	W		TN
	Sarah J.	3	F	W		TN
Guffer,	Isaac	22	M	W	Tenant	TN
Wright,	Isaiah	35	M	W	Tenant	KY
	Sophraniaia	35	F	W		KY
	Elizabeth J.	14	F	W		KY
	William	9	M	W		KY
	Sarah A.	7	F	W		TN
	Pervina	5	F	W		TN
	Freely A.	3	F	W		TN
	Resenia	2	F	W		TN
	Nancy E.	1	F	W		TN
Crabtree,	Pearson M.	35	M	W	Farmer	TN
	Mary A.	34	F	W		TN
	Martha	13	F	W		TN
	Almira	11	F	W		TN
	Wm. M.	9	M	W		TN
	Emeline	7	F	W		TN
	Mortilia	5	F	W		TN
	Pearson	5/12	M	W		TN
Wright,	James M.	43	M	W	Farmer	TN
	Pevina	69	F	W	Domestic	GA
	Freely	30	F	W	Domestic	TN
	Pevina	26	F	W	Domestic	TN
Rains,	Green B.	21	M	W	Day Laborer	KY

1860 Fentress Co. TN Census

Name		Age Remarks	Sex	Race	Profession	Birth Place

Civil District No. 9
Recorded 31 July 1860

Name		Age	Sex	Race	Profession	Birth Place
Young,	John	57	M	W	Farmer	TN
	Louisa	50	F	W		TN
	Lucinda	16	F	W		TN
	John E.	12	M	W		TN
Stephens,	Zorobibel	75	M	W	Farmer	SC
	Susanah	69	F	W		TN
						.
Ramsey,	Samuel	39	M	W	Farmer	TN
	Jeriah	37	F	W		TN
	Mahala	16	F	W		TN
	William G.	13	M	W		TN
	Phebe	10	F	W		TN
	Elmira	6	F	W		TN
	Catharine J.	4	F	W		TN
	James A.	1	M	W		TN
Norris,	Thomas	67	M	W	Farmer	NC
	Kiziah	66	F	W		?
	Jonathan	25	M	W		?
Durham,	James	25	M	W	Farmer	TN
	Louisa	22	F	W		TN
	Lotha J.	3	F	W		TN
	Armilda	1	F	W		TN
Norris,	Alfred	30	M	W	Farmer	NC
	Emeline	32	F	W		TN
	Jemissa	13	F	W		TN
	Sarah	10	F	W		TN
	Squire J.	8	M	W		TN
	Sis.	6	F	W		TN
	Thomas J.	3	M	W		TN
Ramsey,	Robert	35	M	W		TN
	Charlotte	34	F	W		NC
	W. T.	15	M	W		TN
	Kiziah C.	12	F	W		TN
	Charles P.	10	M	W		TN
	Albert C.	8	M	W		TN
	Robert C.	5	M	W		TN
	Calrenna	9/12	F	W		TN

1860 Fentress Co. TN Census

Name		Age Remarks	Sex	Race	Profession	Birth Place

Civil District No. 9
Recorded 31 July 1860

Name		Age Remarks	Sex	Race	Profession	Birth Place
Norris,	Soloman	36	M	W	Farmer	NC
	Milly	33	F	W		TN
	Kiziah	15	F	W		TN
	Jane	12	F	W		TN
	J.	9	F	W		TN
	James T.	6	M	W		TN
	Delphia A.	3	F	W		TN
Adkinson,	Lewis	50	M	W	Farmer	VA
	Ascencia	43	F	W		TN
	Nancy E.	21	F	W		TN
	Francis M.	19	M	W		TN
	William J.	17	M	W		TN
	Elizabeth	15	F	W		TN
	Joel	13	M	W		TN
	Edward W.	12	M	W		TN
	Rebeccah	10	F	W		TN
	Charles E.	8	M	W		TN
	Tennessee	5	F	W		TN
	Lewis W.	3	M	W		TN
Baldwin,	Jesse	22	M	W	Tenant	TN
	Martha A.	25	F	W		TN
	William	5/12	M	W		TN
McNew,	Jesse	27	M	W	Tenant	TN
	Sarah A.	25	F	W		SC
	Lucinda J.	5	F	W		TN
	Margaret L.	3	F	W		TN
	William H.	11/12	M	W		TN
Hoover,	John G.	35	M	F	Farmer	TN
	Sarah	35	F	W		NC
	Nancy E.	16	F	W		TN
	Henry	13	M	W		TN
	James M.	11	M	W		TN
	William R.	9	M	W		TN
	Mary A.	8	F	W		TN
	John	5	M	W		TN
	Unnamed	2	M	W		TN

1860 Fentress Co. TN Census

Name		Age Remarks	Sex	Race	Profession	Birth Place

Civil District No. 9
Recorded 1 Aug. 1860

Name		Age Remarks	Sex	Race	Profession	Birth Place
Garrett,	Elijah	54	M	W	Farmer	VA
	Anna	57	F	W		VA
	John	24	M	W		TN
	Mary	24	F	W		TN
	Martha	15	F	W		TN
	Julia	13	F	W		TN
	Zuchariah	11	M	W		TN
McIran,	Jasper	42	M	W	Day Laborer	VA
Hatfield,	Carroll	27	M	W	Farmer	TN
	Elizabeth	20	F	W		TN
	Martha E.	1	F	W		TN
	William	60	M	W	No Occupation	TN
	Elizabeth	60	F	W		TN
Philips,	Jonathan	32	M	W	Tenant	NC
	Margaret	32	F	W		NC
	James C.	10	M	W		NC
	Nancy C.	8	F	W		NC
	Martha S.	6	F	W		NC
	Eliza J.	4	F	W		NC
	Sarah E.	2	F	W		NC
	John W.	5/12	M	W		NC
Miller,	Alphus J.	32	M	W	Tenant	NC
	Sarah A.	19	F	W		NC
	Rebeccah J.	1	F	W		NC
Jones,	John	37	M	W	Farmer	NC
	Sevina	36	F	W		TN
	William	19	M	W		TN
	Margaret	17	F	W		TN
	Anderson	15	M	W		TN
	Mary	13	F	W		TN
	Green L.	11	M	W		TN
	John	10	M	W		TN
	Scott	9	M	W		TN
	Larkin	8	M	W		TN
	Burton	6	M	W		TN
	Carroll	4	M	W		TN
	Elijah	1	M	W		TN

1860 Fentress Co. TN Census

Name		Age Remarks	Sex	Race	Profession	Birth Place

Name		Age Remarks	Sex	Race	Profession	Birth Place
Smith,	George	47	M	W	Farmer	TN
	Mary	42	F	W		NC
	John	19	M	W		TN
	Charlotte	18	F	W		TN
	Alfred	16	M	W		TN
	Thomas	14	M	W		TN
	David	12	M	W		TN
	Calvin	10	M	W		TN
	Washington	8	M	W		TN
	Nelly?	6	F	W		TN
	Mary J.	3	F	W		TN
Hall,	Andrew J.	32	M	W	Farmer	TN
	Delphia	31	F	W		NC
	Agnes	13	F	W		TN
	Kiziah	11	F	W		TN
	Jonathan J.	8	M	W		TN
	Elisha	6	M	W		TN
	Susan	3	F	W		TN
	Charlotte	7/12	F	W		TN
Jones,	Tolover?	24	M	W	Farmer	TN
	Phebe	23	F	W		TN
	John	4	M	W		TN
	Mary A. M.	2	F	W		TN
Hall,	David	44	M	W	Farmer	TN
	Amanda	32	F	W		TN
	Daniel	12	M	W		TN
	Martha J.	4	F	W		TN
	David E.	2	M	W		TN
	Amanda M.	2/12	F	W		TN
Cooper,	James F.	11	M	W		TN
Garrett,	Shadrack	24	M	W	Tenant	TN
	Sarah	17	F	W		KY
	William	3	M	W		TN

1860 Fentress Co. TN Census

Name		Age Remarks	Sex	Race	Profession	Birth Place

Civil District No. 9
Recorded 1 Aug. 1860

Name		Age Remarks	Sex	Race	Profession	Birth Place
Smith,	Ruth	64	F	W	Farmer	VA
	Louisa	26	F	W		TN
	Catharine	19	F	W		TN
	Ruth S. N. C.	3	F	W		TN
Hall,	Luke	22	M	W	Farmer	TN
	Tabitha J.	21	F	W		TN
	Lewis H.	5	M	W		TN
	David F.	2	M	W		TN
	Sarah R.	7/12	F	W		TN
	Allen H.	16	M	W	Day Laborer	TN

Recorded 2 Aug. 1860

Name		Age Remarks	Sex	Race	Profession	Birth Place
McFarland,	Elizabeth	46	F	W	Cooper	TN
	Rhoda	23	F	W		TN
	Alexander	21	M	W		TN
	William A.	19	M	W		TN
	Elizabeth A.	17	F	W		TN
	Barbara J.	15	F	W		TN
	Martha T.	12	F	W		TN
	Rebeccah E.	9	F	W		TN
	Elyisa H.	8	F	W		TN
	William T.	8/12	M	W		TN
	Robert A.	8/12	M	W		TN
Wood,	Mathew C.	26	M	W	Farmer	TN
	Dilleny F.	22	F	W		TN
Beaty,	William I.	67	M	W	Farmer	TN
	Martha	63	F	W		TN
	George W.	27	M	W		TN
	Jane	23	F	W		TN
	John M.	21	M	W		TN
	Emeline	16	F	W		TN
Davis,	Joshua	34	M	W	Day Laborer	TN
	Rhoda	11	F	W		TN
	Benjamin	9	M	W		KY

1860 Fentress Co. TN Census

Name		Age Remarks	Sex	Race	Profession	Birth Place
Young,	William	30	M	W		TN
	Nancy	29	F	W		TN
	George	6	M	W		TN
	Mastilba	4	F	W		TN
	Pamela	2	F	W		TN

Civil District No. 9
Recorded 2 Aug. 1860

1860 Fentress Co. TN Census

Name		Age Remarks	Sex	Race	Profession	Birth Place

Civil District No. 10
Recorded 7 Aug. 1860

Name		Age	Sex	Race	Profession	Birth Place
Brown,	James	35	M	W	Farmer	TN
	Sarah	37	F	W		NC
	Thomas D.	15	M	W	Farmer	TN
	James A.	13	M	W		TN
	William	12	M	W		TN
	Sarah A.	11	F	W		TN
	Ruthey	8	F	W		TN
	Mary A.	5	F	W		TN
	Elizabeth	2	F	W		TN
Anderson,	Lewis	77	M	W	Farmer	NC
	Sarah	75	F	W		NC
Philip,	Alfred	38	M	W	Tenant	TN
	Jane	29	F	W		TN
	Sarah	16	F	W		TN
	Robert	14	M	W		TN
	Elizabeth	11	F	W		TN
	John	9	M	W		TN
	Lavina	3	F	W		TN
	William N.	8/12	M	W		TN
Williams,	W. N.	47	M	W	Farmer	TN
	Sarah	46	F	W		NC
	Mary N.	16	F	W		TN
	Lucy	14	F	W		TN
	Sarah	12	F	W		TN
	Reta	10	F	W		TN
	Eliza	8	F	W		TN
	Emeline	6	F	W		TN
	Amanda	4	F	W		TN
	Samantha	2	F	W		TN
	Mathas	72	M	W	Carpenter	VA
Hull,	G. W.	20	M	W	Tenant	TN
	Martha	18	F	W		TN

1860 Fentress Co. TN Census

Name		Age Remarks	Sex	Race	Profession	Birth Place

Civil District No. 10
Recorded 7 Aug. 1860

Name		Age	Sex	Race	Profession	Birth Place
Smith,	William	61	M	W	Tenant	TN
	Lucinda	24	F	W		TN
	Alexander	18	M	W		TN
	Tennessee	16	F	W		TN
	Mary A.	13	F	W		TN
	Daniel	85	M	W	Cooper	VA
	Mary	80	F	W		VA
Evans,	Samuel	33	M	W	Farmer	TN
	Deborah	36	F	W		TN
	Abigail H.	7	F	W		TN
	John P.	3	M	W		TN
	David	1	M	W		TN
Price,	John M.	52	M	W	Farmer	TN
	Mary	54	F	W		TN
	Elizabeth A.	21	F	W		TN
	Alvin C.	15	M	W	Farmer	TN
	Joseph M.	13	M	W		TN
Range,	James T.	31	M	W	Farmer	TN
	Mary J.	27	F	W		TN
	Eliza A.	4	F	W		TN
	Alfred J.	1	M	W		TN
Buck,	Eliza	46	F	W	Domestic	TN
	William	24	M	W	Farmer	TN
	Landon	20	M	W	Farmer	TN
	Noah	14	M	W		TN
	John	22	M	W	Farmer	TN
Tompkins,	James M.	31	M	W	Farmer	TN
	Melinda	29	F	W		TN
	Mary J. E.	10	F	W		TN
	George J. E.	8	M	W		TN
	William D.	6	M	W		TN
	Louisa C.	4	F	W		KY
	Sarah A.	1	F	W		TN

1860 Fentress Co. TN Census

Name		Age Remarks	Sex	Race	Profession	Birth Place

Civil District No. 10
Recorded 7 Aug. 1860

Name		Age Remarks	Sex	Race	Profession	Birth Place
Anderson,	Eason	39	M	W	Farmer	NC
	Dice	42	F	W		NC
	Rhoda	16	F	W		TN
	William	14	M	W		TN
	Nelson	12	M	W		TN
	Thompson	9	M	W		TN
Brewster,	John	35	M	W	Farmer	TN
	Rebeccah	34	F	W		KY
	Jesse	11	M	W		TN
	William S.	8	M	W		TN
	James T.	7	M	W		TN
	Feriba	5	F	W		TN
	Jasper N.	1	M	W		TN
Anderson,	Thomas	44	M	W	Farmer	NC
	Pennah	40	F	W		NC
	Lewis	19	M	W	Farmer	TN
	Arthur	15	M	W	Farmer	TN
	Robert	13	M	W		TN
	Charles A.	10	M	W		TN
	Ellis	6	M	W		TN
	George W.	3	M	W		TN
	James A.	1	M	W		TN
Abbott,	Kiziah	28	F	W	Domestic	TN
Sewell,	Jesse	59	M	W	Farmer	TN
	Nancy	57	F	W		TN
	Stephen J.	20	M	W	Farmer	TN
	Jesse F.	15	M	W	Farmer	TN
Bow,	Henry	30	M	W	Farmer	KY
	Elizabeth C.	31	F	W		TN
	Nancy A. E.	1	F	W		KY
	Sarah F.	15 days	F	W		TN

1860 Fentress Co. TN Census

Name		Age Remarks	Sex	Race	Profession	Birth Place

Civil District No. 10
Recorded 7 Aug. 1860

Name		Age Remarks	Sex	Race	Profession	Birth Place
Anderson,	Lewis	43	M	W	Farmer	NC
	Genlia	38	F	W		NC
	Marshal	21	M	W	Day Laborer	NC
	Eason	20	M	W	Day Laborer	TN
	William	17	M	W	Day Laborer	TN
	James R.	15	M	W	Day Laborer	TN
	Matilda J.	10	F	W		TN
	James A.	5	M	W		TN
	Mary S.	2	F	W		TN
	Nancy A.	5/12	F	W		TN

Recorded 8 Aug. 1860

Name		Age Remarks	Sex	Race	Profession	Birth Place
Edwards,	William N.	65	M	W	Farmer	NC
	Rhoda	64	F	W		NC
Norman,	James	25	M	W	Farmer	TN
	Elizabeth	18	F	W		KY
	Jesse F.	1	M	W		TN
Bow,	Squire	40	M	W	Farmer	KY
	Matilda J.	36	F	W		TN
	William A.	10	M	W		KY
	Mary C.	8	F	W		KY
	Martha H.	7	F	W		KY
	Jesse F.	5	M	W		KY
	Nancy E.	1	F	W		KY
Brown,	Thomas	57	M	W	Farmer	TN
	Mary	61	F	W		TN
	George W.	20	M	W		KY
Spoch,	Nancy	12	F	W		TN

1860 Fentress Co. TN Census

Name		Age Remarks	Sex	Race	Profession	Birth Place

Civil District No. 10
Recorded 8 Aug. 1860

Name		Age	Sex	Race	Profession	Birth Place
Hull,	Allen B.	48	M	W	Farmer	KY
	Irene	43	F	W		NC
	William P.	19	M	W	Farmer	TN
	Mary E.	17	F	W		TN
	Nathaniel R.	15	M	W	Farmer	TN
	Franklin D.	13	M	W		TN
	Qui C.	10	M	W		TN
	Enoch S.	9	M	W		TN
	Lewis A.	7	M	W		TN
	John R.	6	M	W		TN
	Delia H.	3	F	W		TN
	Anderson Y.	5/12	M	W		TN
Sewell,	A. W.	23	M	W	Farmer	TN
	Tabitha	22	F	W		TN
	Royetta	4	F	W		TN
	Selina N.	2	F	W		TN
	Francis M.	9/12	M	W		TN
Welch,	Elijah	68	M	W	Farmer	VA
	Catharine	55	F	W		NC
	David F.	22	M	W	Cooper	KY
	Elizabeth E.	18	F	W		KY
	Nancy M.	16	F	W		KY
	George W.	13	M	W		KY
	Jonathan	11	M	W		TN
Abbott,	Susanah	9	F	W		KY
Price,	Samuel B.	27	M	W	Farmer	TN
	Mary A.	29	F	W		TN
	James M.	3	M	W		KY
	Sarah E.	2	F	W		TN
	William E.	11/12	M	W		TN
Welch,	I. D.	30	M	W	Farmer	KY
	Sarah	20	F	W		TN

1860 Fentress Co. TN Census

Name		Age Remarks	Sex	Race	Profession	Birth Place

Civil District No. 10
Recorded 8 Aug. 1860

Name		Age	Sex	Race	Profession	Birth Place
Good,	John	42	M	W		TN
	Lentice	39	F	W		TN
	Aaron	19	M	W	Farmer	TN
	Margaret	18	F	W		TN
	Joseph	14	M	W		TN
	Elizabeth	10	F	W		TN
	Mary J.	9	F	W		TN
	Jeremiah	7	M	W		TN
	Martha	5	F	W		TN
	Lucinda	3	F	W		TN
Good,	William	20	M	W	Tenant	TN
	Sarah A.	21	F	W		TN
	Marilda E.	1/12	F	W		TN
Tompkins,	Alexander	47	M	W	Farmer	TN
	Rebeccah	47	F	W		TN
	William	19	M	W	Farmer	TN
	Lyia	17	F	W		TN
	Calvin	10	M	W		TN
	Margaret E.	7	F	W		TN
	Granville	4	M	W		TN
	Mary A.	11/12	F	W		TN
	Rebeccah A.	1	F	W		TN
Burden,	George W.	24	M	W	Farmer	TN
	Nancy J.	28	F	W		TN
	Joseph A.	7	M	W		KY
	James G.	5	M	W		KY
	Eliza	2	F	W		TN
	Esther	76	F	W	Domestic	SC
Loveless,	John	54	M	W	Farmer	KY
	Lucinda	23	F	W		TN
	Thomas J.	4	M	W		KY
	William H.	2	M	W		TN
Looper,	Hiley	13	F	W		KY

1860 Fentress Co. TN Census

Name		Age	Sex	Race	Profession	Birth
		Remarks				
						Place

Civil District No. 10
Recorded 8 Aug. 1860

Name		Age	Sex	Race	Profession	Birth Place
Stepp,	James	49	M	W	Farmer	NC
	Elizabeth	57	F	W		NC
	John A. S.	17	M	W	Farmer	NC
Christian,	Eliza	33	F	W	Domestic	TN
	Silina	13	F	W		TN
	Rufus	8	M	W		TN
	Alvin	6	M	W		TN
Stepp,	Mary A.	18	F	W	Domestic	TN
	Preston	20	M	W	Farmer	TN

Recorded 9 Aug. 1860

Name		Age	Sex	Race	Profession	Birth Place
Wright,	Mathew	34	M	W	Tenant	TN
	Nancy	37	F	W		TN
	Elizabeth J.	8	F	W		TN
	Sarah M.	6	F	W		TN
	John L.	5	M	W		TN
	Mary A.	3	F	W		TN
	Lenial S.	4/12	M	W		TN
Adkins,	William	33	M	W	Farmer	TN
	Nancy	33	F	W		TN
	Levina	10	F	W		TN
	Wyatt	8	M	W		TN
	Enwill	6	M	W		TN
	Mary	4	F	W		TN
	Francis M.	2	M	W		TN
	Sarah	8/12	F	W		TN
Ellis,	Edward	37	M	W	Farmer	TN
	Jane	37	F	W		TN
	Sarah	19	F	W		TN
	James	18	M	W	Farmer	TN
	Susan	16	M	W	Farmer	TN
	Martin V.	14	M	W		TN
	Edward	13	M	W		TN
	Abanna	9	F	W		TN
	Calaway	5	M	W		TN
	Parizida	4	F	W		TN
	Lavinia J.	1	F	W		TN

1860 Fentress Co. TN Census

Name		Age Remarks	Sex	Race	Profession	Birth Place

Civil District No. 10
Recorded 9 Aug. 1860

Name		Age	Sex	Race	Profession	Birth Place
Luckey,	Richard R.	27	M	W	Farmer	NC
	Margaret	26	F	W		IN
	Sarah E.	1	F	W		TN
Daughaty,	William	40	M	W	Farmer	TN
	Catharine	36	F	W		KY
	John	19	M	W	Farmer	TN
	Mary	18	F	W		TN
	Lucinda	16	F	W		TN
Cobb,	Jesse Sr.	69	M	W	Farmer	SC
	Elizabeth	28	F	W		GA
Johnson,	Firiba	12	F	W		GA
	Sarah C.	10	F	W		GA
	Anella	4	F	W		KY
Cobb,	Delilah M.	2	F	W		TN
Smith,	Richard	43	M	W	Farmer	TN
	Hulda	46	F	W		TN
	William	20	M	W	Farmer	TN
	Jesse	18	M	W	Farmer	TN
	Samuel	15	M	W	Farmer	TN
	Thomas	12	M	W		TN
	Joshua	8	M	W		TN
Hill,	Lewis	37	M	W	Tenant	TN
	Louisa	36	F	W		TN
	David	19	M	W	Tenant	TN
	Susanah J.	13	F	W		TN
	Mary	11	F	W		TN
	Dilley	9	F	W		TN
	John	5	M	W		TN
	Isaac	2	M	W		TN
	Nancy	6/12	F	W		TN

1860 Fentress Co. TN Census

Name		Age Remarks	Sex	Race	Profession	Birth Place

Civil District No. 10
Recorded 10 Aug. 1860

Name		Age	Sex	Race	Profession	Birth Place
Lewallin,	John	22	M	W	Farmer	TN
	Mary	17	F	W		TN
Paul,	James F.	38	M	W	Farmer	VA
	Mary N.	32	F	W		TN
	Martin L.	13	M	W		TN
	Sarah J.	5	F	W		TN
Walker,	Jane	66	F	W	Domestic	VA
	Margaret J.	35	F	W	Domestic	TN
Bruce,	Dice	29	F	W	Gardening	TN
	Nancy J.	7	F	W		TN
	John M.	6	M	W		TN
	Elizabeth J.	3	F	W		TN

1860 Fentress Co. TN Census

Name		Age Remarks	Sex	Race	Profession	Birth Place

Civil District No. 11
Recorded 1 June 1860

Name		Age	Sex	Race	Profession	Birth Place
Manis,	James	36	M	W	Farmer	IL
	Ruhania	34	F	W		TN
	John	17	M	W	Farmer	IL
	Susan	12	F	W		TN
	James M.	10	M	W		TN
	Isaac	8	M	W		TN
	Mary M.	5	F	W		TN
	William C.	3	M	W		TN
	Downs D.	7/12	M	W		TN
Whited,	Susanah	74	F	W	Domestic	VA
Combs,	James H.	38	M	W	Farmer	TN
	Lucy	40	F	W		TN
	George W.	15	M	W	Farmer	TN
	Thomas C.	13	M	W		TN
	Cinthia	10	F	W		TN
	Clrinary A.	8	F	W		TN
	James A.	3	M	W		TN
	Theophalus	10/12	M	W		TN
Padgett,	James	49	M	W	Farmer	TN
	Alcy	54	F	W		TN
	John	18	M	W		KY
	Francis M.	15	M	W		TN
Garratt,	Henderson	49	M	W	Farmer Tenant	TN
	Elizabeth	45	F	W		TN
	John	29	M	W		TN
	Bramlette	23	M	W		TN
	Nancy	19	F	W		TN
	William	15	M	W		TN
	George	13	M	W		TN
	Greenberry	12	M	W		TN
	Bethia	8	F	W		TN
Garratt,	James H.	28	M	W	Farmer	TN
	Mahala	25	F	W		TN

1860 Fentress Co. TN Census

Name		Age Remarks	Sex	Race	Profession	Birth Place

Civil District No. 11
Recorded 1 June 1860

Name		Age	Sex	Race	Profession	Birth Place
Fowler,	Nancy	67	F	W	Domestic	TN
	Patsey	43	F	W		TN
	John	32	M	W	Farmer	TN
	Elander J.	23	F	W	Domestic	TN
	Martha F.	14	F	W		TN
	James H.	11	M	W		TN
Fowler,	William	36	M	W	Farmer	NC
	Thursa	25	F	W		TN
	Sampson	8	M	W		TN
	John A.	5	M	W		TN
	Benjamin	1	M	W		TN
Garratt,	Louisa	60	F	W	Farming	NC
Bird,	Campbell	29	M	W	Farmer	TN
	Hannah	25	F	W		TN
	Lewis	1	M	W		TN
Beaty,	Philip	43	M	W	Farmer	TN
	Mary A.	38	F	W		TN
	Eliza M.	19	F	W		TN
	Hannah	14	F	W		TN
	Margaret	12	F	W		TN
	Mary	10	F	W		TN
	Haley	8	M	W		TN
	David	7	M	W		TN
	Isaac	5	M	W		TN
	Samantha	8/12	F	W		TN
Bird,	Andrew	51	M	W	Farmer	TN
	James	12	M	W		TN
	Elbert	9	M	W		TN
Garratt,	Mary	29	F	W		TN
	Andrew J.	1	M	W		TN

1860 Fentress Co. TN Census

Name		Age Remarks	Sex	Race	Profession	Birth Place

Civil District No. 11
Recorded 1 June 1860

Name		Age	Sex	Race	Profession	Birth Place
Greer,	Thomas	44	M	W	Farmer	TN
	Rachel	35	F	W		TN
	Clementine	15	F	W		TN
	James	13	M	W		TN
	John	11	M	W		TN
	Armilda	9	F	W		TN
	Mary A.	6	F	W		TN
	David	5	M	W		FN
	Thomas	2	M	W		TN
Beaty,	Andrew J.	29	M	W	Farmer	KY
	Jane	25	F	W		TN
	John A.	1/12	M	W		TN
Reagan,	Samuel	49	M	W		NC
	Elizabeth	55	F	W		KY
	John M.	23	M	W		TN
Beaty,	Sevena	22	F	W		TN
	Nancy J.	1	F	W		TN
Smith,	George	37	M	W	Farmer	TN
	Juda	26	F	W		TN
	John	13	M	W		TN
	Mary	10	F	W		TN
	Abraham	9	M	W		TN
	Elijah	5	M	W		TN
	Margaret	3	F	W		TN
	James A.	11/12	M	W		TN
Donaldson,	Edward	36	M	W	Coal Miner	England
	Rosa Ann	26	F	W		OH
	Thomas	9	M	W		KY
Donaldson,	Charles	35	M	W	Miner	England
	Ann	37	F	W		England
	Sarah	4	F	W		OH
	Robert W.	2	M	W		KY
	Elizabeth	7/12	F	W		TN

1860 Fentress Co. TN Census

Name		Age Remarks	Sex	Race	Profession	Birth Place

Civil District No. 11
Recorded 1 June 1860

Name		Age	Sex	Race	Profession	Birth Place
Donaldson,	Robert	23	M	W	Miner	England
	Mlda	22	F	W		KY
	John	7/12	M	W		TN
Conatser,	Morgan	39	M	W	Farmer	TN
	Mary	35	F	W		TN
	Margaret J.	15	F	W		TN
	Balaam	13	M	W		TN
	Scott	12	M	W		TN
	Francis M.	11	M	W		TN
	Melissa	8	F	W		TN
	Winton B.	6	M	W		TN
	Martha	4	F	W		TN
	Mary	4	F	W		TN
	John	1/12	M	W		TN

Recorded 2 June 1860

Name		Age	Sex	Race	Profession	Birth Place
Reagan,	Charles	60	M	W	Farmer	TN
	John E.	26	M	W	Farmer	TN
	Alexander A.	17	M	W	Farmer	TN
	Charles A.	15	M	W	Farmer	TN
	Lady A.	12	F	W		TN
Dibnell,	Lavina	66	F	W	Domestic	TN
Woolsey,	Isaac G.	31	M	W	Physician	KY
	Emeline C.	28	F	W		TN
	Charles R.	7	M	W		KY
	Adela A. A.	6	F	W		KY
	Constanza I.	4	F	W		TN
Reagan,	James H.	21	M	W	Farmer	TN
	Emeline	23	F	W		TN
Anderson,	John T. Stepson	6	M	W		TN
Reagan,	William F.	3	M	W		TN
	Charles	1	M	W		TN

1860 Fentress Co. TN Census

Name		Age	Sex	Race	Profession	Birth
					Remarks	
						Place

Civil District No. 11
Recorded 2 June 1860

Name		Age	Sex	Race	Profession	Birth Place
Clark,	Abraham	35	M	W	Farmer	TN
	Caroline	37	F	W		TN
	Robert	12	M	W		TN
	Julia A.	10	F	W		TN
	William	8	M	W		TN
	Clamanza E.	11/12	F	W		TN
Beaty,	Allen	42	M	W	Farmer	KY
	Mary	39	F	W		TN
	James	16	M	W		TN
	George M. D.	14	M	W		TN
	Andrew J.	12	M	W		TN
	Anna	10	F	W		TX
	Pleasant C.	9	M	W		TX
Greer,	David	71	M	W	Farmer	TN
Tucker,	Lucinda	36	F	W	Domestic	TN
	James	16	M	W	Farmer	AR
	Nancy	14	F	W		AR
	Roseana	6	F	W		TN
Poor,	Moses	24	M	W	Farmer	TN
	Parilla	17	F	W		TN
Huddleston,	Philip M.	38	M	W	Farmer	TN
	Esther	40	F	W		TN
	Ambrose J.	16	M	W		TN
	Kiza E.	7	F	W		TN
Buck,	John H.	35	M	W	Farmer	TN
	Ruhama	32	F	W		TN
	Squire	14	M	W		TN
	Thomas	12	M	W		TN
	Clarborne	10	M	W		TN
	Ambrose S.	7	M	W		TN
	James W.	6	M	W		TN
	Julia Ann	3	F	W		TN
	David C.	1	M	W		TN

1860 Fentress Co. TN Census

Name		Age Remarks	Sex	Race	Profession	Birth Place

Civil District No. 11
Recorded 2 June 1860

Name		Age	Sex	Race	Profession	Birth Place
Huddleston,	Lenard C.	53	M	W	Farmer	TN
	Hannah	57	F	W		NC
	David F.	26	M	W	Farmer	TN
	Sibly	20	F	W		TN
	Wiley W.	24	M	W	Farmer	TN
	George W.	22	M	W	Farmer	TN
	Kiza	18	F	W		TN
	Martha A.	16	F	W		TN
	Esther	13	F	W		TN
	Sarah A.	8	F	W		TN
Huddleston,	Thomas S.	50	M	W	Farmer	TN
	Jane	46	F	W		TN
	Thomas L. B.	16	M	W	Farmer	TN
	William E.	14	M	W		TN
	Mary L.	11	F	W		TN
	Cumanza C.	8	F	W		TN
	Abigail	5	F	W		TN
Mare,	David	60	M	W	Farmer	SC
	Esther	48	F	W		TN
	Sarah A.	22	F	W		TN
	Clementine	14	F	W		TN
	James	16	M	W	Farmer	TN
	Robert	8	M	W		TN
	Esther	6	F	W		TN
Mancord,	Burnell	60	M	W	Farmer	NC
	Kyndrick M.	14	M	W		TN
Scrogan,	John G.	33	M	W	Farmer	TN
	Margaret	33	F	W		TN
	Andrew J.	12	M	W		TN
	Amanda J.	10	F	W		TN
	Nina A.	7	F	W		TN
	Feriba	5	F	W		TN
	Melinda	3	F	W		TN
	Mary A.	1	F	W		TN

1860 Fentress Co. TN Census

Name		Age Remarks	Sex	Race	Profession	Birth Place

Civil District No. 11
Recorded 2 June 1860

Name		Age	Sex	Race	Profession	Birth Place
Petty,	John V. H.	31	M	W	Farmer	TN
	Rhoda	28	F	W		TN
Huddleston,	Edward E.	36	M	W	Farmer	TN
	Artemia	32	F	W		TN
	Mary E.	7	F	W		TN
	Bethel C. B.	3	M	W		TN
	Pamila C.	7/12	F	W		TN
	Mary	22	F	W	Domestic	TN
	J. A. B.	21	F	W	Farmer	TN
Richardson,	William	23	M	W	Farmer	KY
	Mary J.	24	F	W		TN
	James Mc	2	M	W		TN
	Artemia	10/12	F	W		TN
Huddleston,	Daniel E.	31	M	W	Farmer	TN
	Elizabeth	25	F	W		KY
	Adam	5	M	W		TN
	Delilah J.	3	F	W		TN
	Killus E.	1	M	W		TN
	Elijah L.	2/12	M	W		TN
Smith,	Russell M.	29	M	W	Farmer	TN
	Lucinda	26	F	W		TN
	Jane	7	F	W		TN
	Margaret	5	F	W		TN
	Mary	4	F	W		TN
	Lucy	1	F	W		TN
Mancord,	Wayman	34	M	W	Farmer	TN
	Amanda	29	F	W		TN
	Gardall	9	M	W		TN
Huddleston,	James A.	26	M	W	Farmer	TN
	Melinda	21	F	W		TN
	Flouin M.	2	M	W		TN

1860 Fentress Co. TN Census

Name		Age Remarks	Sex	Race	Profession	Birth Place

Civil District No. 11
Recorded 2 June 1860

Name		Age Remarks	Sex	Race	Profession	Birth Place
Richardson,	Jeffrey H.	38	M	W	Farmer	TN
	Almira	33	F	W		TN
	Rebeccah A.	10	F	W		TN
	Mary E.	8	F	W		TN
	William H	4	M	W		TN
	John L.	2	M	W		TN
	Samuel	10	M	W		TN
Gentrer,	Jeffrey H	11	M	W		TN
Scott,	James T.	38	M	W	Farmer	NC
	Susanah	30	F	W		TN
	David A.	17	M	W	Farmer	TN
	Matilda E.	16	F	W		TN
	Martha J.	13	F	W		TN
	Mary A.	12	F	W		TN
	Zimanich P.	10	M	W		TN
	Zephaniah L.	7	M	W		TN
	Alexander M.	4	M	W		TN
	Sarah E.	1	F	W		TN
Moon,	Mary J.	27	F	W	Domestic	TN
	James D.	10	M	W		TN
	John A.	8	M	W		TN
	William P.	6	M	W		TN
	Landon C. H.	3	M	W		TN
	Unnamed	6/12	M	W		TN
Beaty,	Pleasant	40	M	W	Farmer	TN
	Mahala	19	F	W		TN
	Margaret	17	F	W		TN
	Abigail	14	F	W		TN
	Catharine	12	F	W		TN
	Cinthia	9	F	W		TN
	Mathew W.	7	M	W		TN
	David	5	M	W		TN
	Alfred K.	2	M	W		TN
	Cinthia	50	F	W	Farming	TN

1860 Fentress Co. TN Census

Name		Age Remarks	Sex	Race	Profession	Birth Place

Civil District No. 11
Recorded 2 June 1860

Name		Age	Sex	Race	Profession	Birth Place
Stanford,	James M.	29	M	W	Farmer	NC
	Anna C.	24	F	W		KY
	Priscilla M.	6	F	W		KY
	Mary M.	5	F	W		KY
	Rally H.	7/12	M	W		KY

Recorded 4 June 1860

Name		Age	Sex	Race	Profession	Birth Place
Wright,	E. D.	33	M	W	Farmer	TN
	Phebe	31	F	W		TN
	Ann E.	6	F	W		TN
	Charles R.	5	M	W		TN
	Margaret A.	10/12	F	W		TN
Clark,	Elijah	37	M	W	Farmer	TN
	Catherine	25	F	W		TN
	Milissa	5	F	W		TN
	Alvin	3	M	W		TN
Whited,	Robert	32	M	W	Farmer	TN
	Vernetta J.	31	F	W		TN
	James R.	12	M	W		TN
	George W.	10	M	W		TN
	John	8	M	W		TN
	Mary A.	6	F	W		TN
	William A.	3	M	W		TN
	Emeline	1	F	W		TN
Clark,	Julia A.	55	F	W	Farming	VA
	Stephen	22	M	W	Farming	TN
	James	20	M	W		TN
	Thomas	19	M	W		TN
	Silas	16	M	W	Farming	TN
	Phebe	13	F	W		TN

1860 Fentress Co. TN Census

Name		Age Remarks	Sex	Race	Profession	Birth Place

Civil District No. 11
Recorded 4 June 1860

Name		Age	Sex	Race	Profession	Birth Place	
Chapman,	Rally	65	M	W	Farmer	VA	
	Priscilla	66	F	W		NC	
	Nancy	35	F	W		VA	
Poe,	Lucy	32	F	W		VA	
Chapman,	Judy	24	F	W		VA	
Poe,	William M.	9	M	W		?	
	Charles H.	7	M	W		?	
Malds,	John	27	M	W	Farmer	TN	
	Mary J.	21	F	W		TN	
	Eliza	1	F	W		TN	
	David	3/12	M	W		TN	
Murphy,	Greenberry	31	M	W	Farmer	KY	
	Charlotte	29	F	W		TN	
	Lucinda A. M. J.	11	F	W		TN	
	John	8	M	W		TN	
	William A.	7	M	W		TN	
	Margaret	1	F	W		TN	
Fowler,	E. R.	27	M	W	Farmer	NC	
	Leah	38	F	W		TN	
	Jeremiah	3	M	W		TN	
	Parazetta	3/12	F	W		TN	
Whited,	Susanah	40	F	W	Farming	TN	
	Louisa J.	19	F	W		TN	
	James V.	17	M	W	Farming	IL	
	William H.	15	M	W	Farming	IL	
	Alfred B.	13	M	W		TN	Deaf & Dumb
	Elizabeth F.	9	F	W		TN	
	Robert T.	5	M	W		TN	
	Mary A.	3	F	W		TN	
	Jesse C.	10/12	M	W		TN	

1860 Fentress Co. TN Census

Name		Age Remarks	Sex	Race	Profession	Birth Place

Civil District No. 11
Recorded 4 June 1860

Name		Age	Sex	Race	Profession	Birth Place
Smith,	Mathew	73	M	W	Farmer	VA
	Izsybella?	56	F	W		VA
	John	34	M	W	Farmer	TN
	Francis M.	16	M	W	Farmer	TN
	Mary	14	F	W		TN
Wright,	John	77	M	W	Miller	MD
	Elizabeth	62	F	W		MD
	Lemuel C.	22	M	W		TN
Soloman,	Sarah	27	F	W		TN
Prisherd,	Thomas	43	M	W	Farmer	TN
	Sarah	45	F	W		TN
	William A.	20	M	W	Farmer	TN
	John E.	18	M	W	Farmer	TN
	Simon W.	16	M	W	Farmer	TN
	Eli B.	14	M	W		TN
	Delilah C.	11	F	W		TN
	Alfred K.	8	M	W		TN
Walker,	Eliza	43	F	W	Domestic	TN
	Jackson M.	7	M	W		TN
Poor,	Calaway	50	M	W	Farming	TN
	Mary	50	F	W		TN
	Jube	15	M	W	Farming	IL
	Wesley W.	14	M	W		TN
	Calvin	11	M	W		TN
	Genetta	9	F	W		TN
Scott,	John	6	M	W		TN
Hill,	William S.	52	M	W	Farmer	TN
	Anna	54	F	W		TN
	Martha E.	21	F	W		TN
	Granville	17	M	W	Farmer	TN
	Lafayette	12	M	W		TN
Gray,	David H.	18	M	W	Farmer	TN
Garrett,	Harriet E.	16	F	W	Domestic	TN
Hill,	Elizabeth	93	F	W	Domestic	VA
	Burton	2	M	W		TN
	Wiley B.	3/12	M	W		TN

140

1860 Fentress Co. TN Census

Name		Age Remarks	Sex	Race	Profession	Birth Place

Civil District No. 11
Recorded 4 June 1860

Name		Age	Sex	Race	Profession	Birth Place
Huckeby,	George	54	M	W	Farming	TN
	Rebeccah	55	F	W		NC
	Feriba	16	F	W		TN
	Amanda	14	F	W		TN
	Andrew J.	19	M	W	Farming	TN
	Armayin	17	F	W		TN
Witt,	Charles W.	36	M	W	Farming	TN
	Phebe E.	34	F	W		TN
	Eliza A.	16	F	W		TN
	Sarah J.	15	F	W		TN
	John A.	11	M	W		TN
	Mary E.	6	F	W		TN
	Martha C.	4	F	W		TN
	Levina E.	1	F	W		TN

Recorded 5 June 1860

Name		Age	Sex	Race	Profession	Birth Place
Poor,	Samuel C.	29	M	W	Farming	TN
	Anes E.	20	F	W		TN
	Mary	3	F	W		TN
Conatser,	Joseph	24	M	W	Farming	TN
	Zerelda J. C.	20	F	W		TN
Price,	Franklin	3	M	W		TN
	Lorenzo D.	1	M	W		TN
Conatser,	Andrew	50	M	W	Farmer	NC
	Mary	47	F	W		TN
	William	23	M	W	Farmer	TN
	Winnie	19	F	W		TN
	Elizabeth	19	F	W		TN
	James K. Polk	15	M	W	Farmer	TN
	George M. Dallas	13	M	W		TN
	Delilah	13	F	W		TN
	Feriba	9	F	W		TN
	Tennessee	7	F	W		TN
	Sharred	28	M	W	Mechanic	TN

1860 Fentress Co. TN Census

Name		Age Remarks	Sex	Race	Profession	Birth Place

Civil District No. 11
Recorded 5 June 1860

Name		Age Remarks	Sex	Race	Profession	Birth Place
Conatser,	Thomas	28	M	W	Farmer	TN
	Mary A.	27	F	W		TN
	Andrew	7	M	W		TN
	Clementine	5	F	W		TN
	Dudley G.	2	M	W		TN
	America J.	7/12	F	W		TN
Gowney,	Timothy	47	M	W	Farming	TN
	Elizabeth	36	F	W		TN
	John	17	M	W	Farming	TN
	Mary E.	14	F	W		TN
	Martha J.	12	F	W		TN
	Samuel	9	M	W		TN
	Nancy L.	7	F	W		TN
	Matilda C.	5	F	W		TN
	William Y.	1	M	W		TN
Scroggin,	George W.	28	M	W	Farmer	IL
	Elizabeth	28	F	W		TN
	Amanda	2	F	W		TN
Cravins,	Henry B.	30	M	W	Farming	TN
	Mary	30	F	W		TN
	Catharine	7	F	W		TN
	George W.	5	M	W		TN
	James P.	2	M	W		TN
Petty,	Joseph	63	M	W	Farmer	TN
	William	21	M	W	Farmer	TN
	Sampson	19	M	W	Farmer	TN
	Mahala	14	F	W		TN
	Melinda	12	F	W		TN
	Lucinda	12	F	W		TN
Davis,	Anderson	45	M	W	Farming	TN
	Lucretia	26	F	W		TN
	Eliza C.	8	F	W		TN
	Izabella	6`	F	W		TN
	Martha J.	2	F	W		TN
	Clarinda E.	8 days	F	W		TN

1860 Fentress Co. TN Census

Name		Age Remarks	Sex	Race	Profession	Birth Place

Civil District No. 11
Recorded 5 June 1860

Name		Age	Sex	Race	Profession	Birth Place
Tucker,	Samuel	20	M	W		TN
	Sarah A.	24	F	W		TN
	Eliza J.	2	F	W		TN
West,	Barliora?	62	F	W	Gardening	TN
	Mary A.	29	F	W		TN
Garratt,	Mary A.	69	F	W	Domestic	TN
Huckeby,	Isham	24	M	W	Farming	TN
	Margaret	19	F	W		TN
	Mary	3	F	W		TN
Riley,	Mary	59	F	W	Domestic	KY
Scroggin,	Robert	32	M	W	Farmer	TN
	Elizabeth	33	F	W		TN
	John M.	12	M	W		TN
	Commodore P.	10	M	W		TN
	Feriba J.	8	F	W		TN
	Esther A.	6	F	W		TN
	Samuel	5	M	W		TN
	Tennessee	3	F	W		TN
	Sarah A.	1	F	W		TN
Crockett,	Joseph M.	30	M	W	Farmer	TN
	Selina J.	25	F	W		TN
	Samantha J.	6	F	W		TN
	Margaret S.	5	F	W		TN
	Serilda A.	3	F	W		TN

1860 Fentress Co. TN Census

Name		Age Remarks	Sex	Race	Profession	Birth Place

Civil District No. 12
Recorded 2 Aug. 1860

Name		Age	Sex	Race	Profession	Birth Place
Ward,	George	46	M	W	Farmer	SC
	Lydia	42	F	W		TN
	William N.	23	M	W	Farmer	TN
	James A.	21	M	W	Farmer	TN
	Mahala	19	F	W		TN
	Richard L.	18	M	W	Farmer	TN
	?	1?	F	W		TN
	Patemar	14	F	W		TN
	?	12	F	W		TN
	Elizabeth	10	F	W		TN
	Winnie	4	F	W		TN
Blakly,	George W.	21	M	W	Day Laborer	TN
Ward,	Sarah	65	F	W	Farmer	VA
	Franky	44	F	W	Farmer	SC
	James	40	M	W	No Occupation	TN
	Eliah	38	M	W	Farmer	TN
Ward,	John	36	M	W	Farmer	TN
	Sarah	26	F	W		TN
	Elizabeth	6	F	W		TN
	Mary	4	F	W		TN
	William	2	M	W		TN
	Martha J.	?/12	F	W		TN
Ward,	John	63	M	W	Farmer	NC
	Elizabeth	54	F	W		TN
	Andrew	20	M	W	Farmer	NC
	Mary	18	F	W		TN
	Caroline	16	F	W		TN
	Jesse	14	M	W		TN
	John W.	12	M	W		TN
	Henry A.	22	M	W		TN

1860 Fentress Co. TN Census

Name		Age Remarks	Sex	Race	Profession	Birth Place

Civil District No. 12
Recorded 2 Aug. 1860

Name		Age	Sex	Race	Profession	Birth Place
Tinch,	Henry F.	33	M	W	Farmer	TN
	Charity	31	F	W		TN
	Desting	10	M	W		TN
	Mary F.	7	F	W		TN
	Andrew J.	3	M	W		TN
	Robert E.	1	M	W		TN
Hurst,	Clarissa	15	F	W	Domestic	TN
Tinch,	Mary A.	75	F	W	No Occupation	SC
Brook,	Thomas W.	28	M	W	Wagoner	NC
	Emma D.	25	F	W		KY
	Mary E.	5	F	W		TN
Davis,	Walter A.	45	M	W	Farmer	TN
	Elizabeth	45	F	W		KY
	Armilda	16	F	W		TN
	Sarah J.	12	F	W		TN
Hoover,	James M.	20	M	W	Farmer	TN
	Artemia	19	F	W		TN
Downs,	Daniel	20	M	W	Day Laborer	TN
	Amity	18	F	W		TN
	Benny	11/12	M	W		TN
Crabtree,	Thomas	60	M	W	Farmer	VA
	Married within					
	Elizabeth	32	F	W		TN the
year						
Crabtree,	William R.	31	M	W	Farmer	TN
	Giney	36	F	W		NC
	Jackson	2	M	W		TN
	Nancy A.	8/12	F	W		TN

Recorded 3 Aug. 1860

Name		Age	Sex	Race	Profession	Birth Place
Davis,	Elizabeth	32	F	W	Farmer	TN
	Bushard	10	M	W		TN
	Pleasant A.	9	M	W		TN
	Melinda J.	6	F	W		TN
	Hannah	3	F	W		TN
	Miles H.	1	M	W		TN
Morgan,	Champton	23	M	W	Day Laborer	TN

1860 Fentress Co. TN Census

Name		Age Remarks	Sex	Race	Profession	Birth Place

Civil District No. 12
Recorded 3 Aug. 1860

Name		Age	Sex	Race	Profession	Birth Place
Howard,	Joseph	46	M	W	Farmer	TN
	Martha	42	F	W		KY
	William	14	M	W		TN
	Burton B.	12	M	W		TN
	Hariet T.	8	F	W		TN
Norman,	Nathaniel	51	M	W	Farmer	TN
	Susanah	46	F	W		TN
	Lary A.	23	F	W		TN
	Frances M.	16	F	W		TN
	Eli L.	17	M	W	Farmer	TN
	William	14	M	W		TN
	Lucinda	11	F	W		TN
	Elizabeth	9	F	W		TN
	Nathan J.	6	M	W		TN
	Filbert C.	4	M	W		TN
	Martha S.	5/12	F	W		TN
Downs,	Shadrach	38	M	W	Farmer	NC
	Nancy	32	F	W		TN
	Thomas	16	M	W		TN
	Wiley	13	M	W		TN
	Sarah	11	F	W		TN
	Panlina	7	F	W		TN
	Margaret	6	F	W		TN
	Lewis	3	M	W		TN
	Churchwell	7/12	M	W		TN
Downs,	Fracia	64	F	W	Tenant	NC
	Lewis	23	M	W		TN
Anderson,	William	39	M	W	Farmer	NC
	Sarah	29	F	W		NC
	Andrew J.	14	M	W		TN
	Sarah J.	11	F	W		TN
	Elizabeth	9	F	W		TN
	William H.	6	M	W		TN
	Raena C.	4	F	W		TN

1860 Fentress Co. TN Census

Name		Age Remarks	Sex	Race	Profession	Birth Place

Civil District No. 12
Recorded 3 Aug. 1860

Name		Age	Sex	Race	Profession	Birth Place
Downs,	Fredric	29	M	W	Farmer	NC
	Lydia	29	F	W		TN
	Leander J.	11	M	W		TN
	Wiley W.	9	M	W		TN
	Mary E.	8	F	W		TN
	Nancy O.	6	F	W		TN
	Mary A.	5	F	W		TN
	Frederic	3	M	W		TN
	Milly	2/12	F	W		TN
Johnson,	Stephen	62	M	W	Farmer	NC
	Anna	56	F	W		NC
	Frances A.	6	F	W		TN
Hicks,	Joseph	20	M	W	Day Laborer	TN
	Elizabeth E.	19	F	W		TN
Fulton,	Daniel	30	M	W	Farmer	TN
	Holly	25	F	W		TN
	Stephen B.	4	M	W		TN
	Nancy A.	5/12	F	W		TN
Rodes,	Ezikeal	44	M	W	Carpenter	NY
	Sarah J.	31	F	W		NY
	Samantha	10	F	W		NY
	Thaddus	8	M	W		NY
	Eugene	4	M	W		NY

Recorded 4 Aug. 1860

Name		Age	Sex	Race	Profession	Birth Place
Tinch,	A.	50	M	W	Farmer	VA
	Winnie	43	F	W		TN
	Jack P.	11	M	W		TN

1860 Fentress Co. TN Census

Name		Age Remarks	Sex	Race	Profession	Birth Place	

Civil District No. 12
Recorded 4 Aug. 1860

Name		Age Remarks	Sex	Race	Profession	Birth Place	
Downs,	Edward	36	M	W	Farmer	NC	
	Anna	32	F	W		TN	
	Anderson	10	M	W		TN	
	Narsissa	8	F	W		TN	
	William	6	M	W		TN	
	John	4	M	W		TN	
	Isaac	3	M	W		TN	
	Redin	6/12	M	W		TN	
Edwards,	Z. B.	33	M	W	Day Laborer	NC	
	Elizabeth	26	F	W		TN	
	Henry S.	10	M	W		TN	
	William A.	9	M	W		TN	
	Mary	7	F	W		TN	
	Lucinda J.	5	F	W		TN	
	John A.	3	M	W		TN	
	Sarah B.	1/12	F	W		TN	
Voiles,	William	38	M	W	Farmer	TN	
	Elizabeth	39	F	W		TN	
	Enoch	16	M	W		TN	
	Penelope	14	F	W		TN	
	James	12	M	W		TN	
	Francis	9	M	W		TN	
	Philip	8	M	W		TN	
Edward,	William A.	27	M	W	Farmer	TN	
	Sarah A.	19	F	W		TN	
	N. A. M.	3/12	F	W		TN	
Otterson,	Franklin	21	M	W	Tenant	VA	
	Henry	23	M	W	Tenant	VA	
	John B.	25	M	W	Tenant	VA	Deaf
	Martha J.	14	F	W		VA	
Otterson,	?	50	F	W	Gardening	VA	

1860 Fentress Co. TN Census

Name		Age Remarks	Sex	Race	Profession	Birth Place

Civil District No. 12
Recorded 4 Aug. 1860

Otterson,	William J.	35	M	W	Farmer	SC
	Emily	24	F	W		TN
	Mary A.	4	F	W		TN

Recorded 6 Aug. 1860

Edward,	Arthur	72	M	W	Farmer	NC
Hicks,	Jesse	52	M	W	Farmer	TN
	Mary	50	F	W		VA
	William	22	M	W	Farmer	TN
	Francis M.	18	M	W	Farmer	TN
	Thomas	16	M	W	Farmer	TN
	Sarah	14	F	W		TN
	Mary	12	F	W		TN
	Jesse	8	M	W		TN
Gentry,	William J.	44	M	W	Farmer	TN
	Sarah	42	F	W		KY
	John	18	M	W	Farmer	TN
	Artemia	11	F	W		TN
	Jesse	4	M	W		TN
Downs,	Jesse	18	M	W	Farmer	TN
	Elizabeth	14	F	W		TN
Brooks,	P. G.	54	F	W	Farmer	NC
	Rhoda	15	F	W		TN
	Lovana F.	13	F	W		TN
	Sinchrillan A.	11	F	W		TN
	Louisa A.	7	M	W		TN
	Alvin P.	5	M	W		TN
	Matilda	2	F	W		TN

1860 Fentress Co. TN Census

Name		Age Remarks	Sex	Race	Profession	Birth Place
Anderson,	John	47	M	W	Farmer	NC
	Sarah	40	F	W		TN
	William L.	19	M	W		TN
	John	16	M	W	Farmer	TN
	Sarah E.	15	F	W		TN
	Martin V. B.	13	M	W		TN
	Eli G.	12	M	W		TN
	David	9	M	W		TN
	James	9	M	W		TN
	William	7	M	W		TN
	Roena	4	F	W		TN
	Cami	1	F	W		TN

Recorded 7 Aug. 1860

Name		Age Remarks	Sex	Race	Profession	Birth Place
Armstrong,	John	31	M	W	Farmer	Ireland
	Sarah	30	F	W		VA
Smith,	William	76	M	W Tenant	NC	
	Mary	70	F	W	SC	
Johnson,	Jane	14	F	W	KY	
	Nancy A.	11	F	W	KY	
Dishman,	Mark	53	M	W	Farmer	NC
	Serilda	47	F	W		NC
	George	21	M	W	Farmer	TN
	William J.	16	M	W	Farmer	TN
	Francis E.	15	F	W		TN
	Serilda E.	12	F	W		TN
	Henry C.	9	M	W		TN
Johnson,	Philip S.	26	M	W	Tenant	TN
	Susanah	23	F	W		TN
	William L.	5	M	W		TN
	Rhoda	3	F	W		TN
	Andrew	4/12	M	W		TN

1860 Fentress Co. TN Census

Name		Age Remarks	Sex	Race	Profession	Birth Place

Civil District No. 12
Recorded 7 Aug. 1860

Name		Age Remarks	Sex	Race	Profession	Birth Place
Trail,	James	26	M	W	Farmer	TN
	Sarah E.	26	F	W		TN
	John H.	5	M	W		TN
	Martha J.	2	F	W		TN
Trail,	Archabald	83	M	W	Tenant	VA
	Nancy	70	F	W		VA
	John	21	M	W	Farmer	TN
	Margaret	18	F	W		TN
Voiles,	Jacob	8	M	W		TN
Brown,	William P.	21	M	W	Farmer	KY
	Nancy	21	F	W		TN
	Mary J.	2	F	W		TN
Brooks,	William S.	20	M	W	Tenant	TN
	Nancy H.	20	F	W		TN
	Lucinda	7/12	F	W		TN
Brooks,	Moses	62	M	W	Farmer	NC
	Feriba	62	F	W		NC
Pade?,	Winnie	1	F	W		NC
Wright,	Wisley	23	M	W	Farmer	KY
	Nancy	25	F	W		NC
Pearson,	James	6	M	W		TN
	Green	5	M	W		TN
	Alfred	3	M	W		TN
Wright,	Tenice	4 Days	F	W		TN
Queen,	E. B.	23	M	W	Farmer	TN
	Nancy J.	22	F	W		TN
	Isaac T.	1	M	W		TN

1860 Fentress Co. TN Census

Name		Age Remarks	Sex	Race	Profession	Birth Place

Civil District No. 12
Recorded 7 Aug. 1860

Name		Age	Sex	Race	Profession	Birth Place
Voiles,	William	31	M	W	Farmer	TN
	Elizabeth	47	F	W		TN
	William S.	18	M	W		TN
	Jonathan H.	16	M	W		TN
	Lyia M.	14	F	W		TN
	George W.	12	M	W		TN
	Rebeccah A.	8	F	W		TN
	John B.	6	M	W		TN
	Daniel F.	2	M	W		TN
Williams,	Elander	70	F	W	Domestic	TN

1860 Fentress Co. TN Census

Index

Abbott	123,125
Abston	53,54
Adkins	29,38,58,107,127
Adkinson	63,107,116
Albertson	1,11,12,13,22,23,38,39
Alexander	61
Allen	69
Alred	36,51
Anderson	121,123,124,133,146,150
Angilly	86
Armstrong	150
Ashburn	54,55,56
Baily	7,43
Baldwin	116
Bales	42
Balwin	54
Bayter	70
Beason	63
Beaty	4,5,6,7,9,10,17,18,31,34,37,59,60,119,131,132,134,137
Benton	4
Bird	131
Birk	92
Birton	84
Blakely	107
Blakly	3,144
Bledsoe	2,3,43
Bledson	57
Block	11
Boles	52
Bond	65
Bookout	82
Bow	123,124
Bowden	9
Bowdon	47,58
Brewster	123
Brock	65,76
Bronniss	22,23,25
Brook	145
Brooks	149,151
Brown	43,63,85,98,121,124,151
Bruce	12,33,129
Bruster	62
Buch	65
Buck	70,71,83,85,122,134
Burden	126

1860 Fentress Co. TN Census

Index

1860 Fentress Co. TN Census

Index

Doss	23,61,64
Dowdy	78
Downs	145,146,147,148,149
Duncan	82,107
Durham	115
Edward	148,149
Edwards	99,124,148
Ellis	127
Eppison	39
Erwin	3
Evans	84,85,88,93,98,106,110,122
Evens	71,72,74,75
Felkins	67
Ferrell	10
Findley	22
Fite	83
Flowers	28,71,75,77
Fowler	131,139
Francis	98
Franklin	4,14,15,20,47,52,58
Frogge	69,72,81,104,110
Fulton	49,147
Gains	70
Gallaway	40
Garratt	130,131,143,117,118,140
Gatewood	41
Gaudin	3
Gennings	105,106
Gentrer	137
Gentry	149
Gilreath	87
Good	126
Gooding	19
Gould	38
Gowney	58,142
Gray	3,25,111,140
Green	83
Greer	30,132,134
Gregory	102
Griden	51
Griffin	83
Guffer	114
Gunning	67
Gunter	17,53
Hair	68

1860 Fentress Co. TN Census

Index

Index

Lastre	68
Latham	102,107
Lavender	42
Lawhorn	95
Ledbetter	15,16,53
Lee	1,2,58
Lewallin	25,129
Linder	6,9
Litterd	73
Livingston	39,89
Livington	2
Locher	84
Lockett	64
Looper	126
Loveless	126
Luckey	128
Mace	32
Malds	139
Manard	92
Mancord	135,136
Manis	130
Mare	135
Massingill	31
Mathas	30,36
McClellon	29
McCollumn	25
McDonnald	73
McFarland	112,119
McFarlin	101
McGee	40,41,42,60
McGinnis	113
McIran	117
McKinny	62
McNew	116
Miller	63,108,111,112,117
Millsap	27
Millsaps	87
Moat	41
Moles	81
Moody	47,48,88
Moon	137
Moredock	70
Morgan	2,113,145
Mullinix	7,26,28,35,81
Murphy	139

1860 Fentress Co. TN Census

Index

1860 Fentress Co. TN Census

Index